The Lives and Ministries of
ELIJAH and ELISHA

Unless otherwise noted, all Scripture quotations are taken from the New American Standard Bible. Nashville: Thomas Nelson Publishers, 1978; the Complete Jewish Bible, Baltimore: Messianic Jewish Publishers, 1998; or the New International Version Bible, New York: International Bible Society, 2002.

Printed in the United States of America

Special thanks to Brian A. Kaiser
for creating the maps showing the travels of Elijah and Elisha.

Cover design by Lisa Rubin,
Messianic Jewish Publishers
Graphic Design by Yvonne Vermillion,
Magic Graphix, Westfork, Arkansas

2019   1

ISBN 978-1-73393-544-9
Library of Congress Control Number:2019944024

Published by:
Lederer Books
An imprint of Messianic Jewish Publishers
6120 Day Long Lane
Clarksville, MD 21029

Distributed by:
Messianic Jewish Publishers & Resources
Order line: (800) 410-7367
lederer@messianicjewish.net
www.MessianicJewish.net

The Lives and Ministries of
ELIJAH and ELISHA

Demonstrating The
Wonderful Power of the Word Of God

Walter C. Kaiser, Jr.

Lederer Books
An imprint of
Messianic Jewish Publishers
Clarksville, MD 21029

Dedicated to:

LEO AND SHIRLEY MILLS

Supervisors Extraordinaire on BSF Tours to Israel

Reference Maps

Elijah

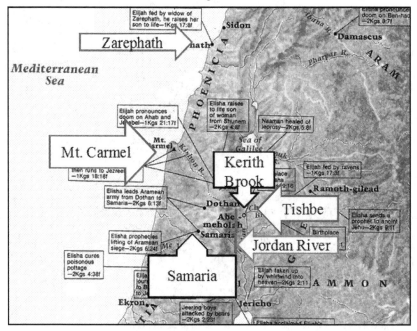

His People

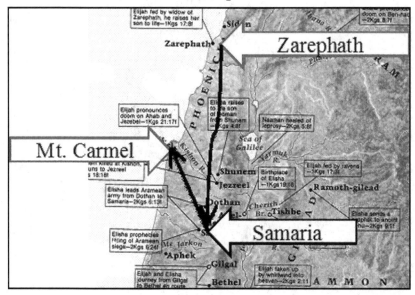

Elijah's Flight

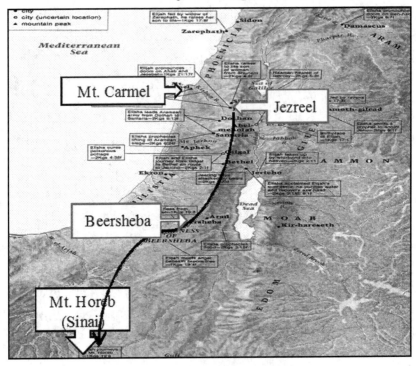

Elijah's Departure

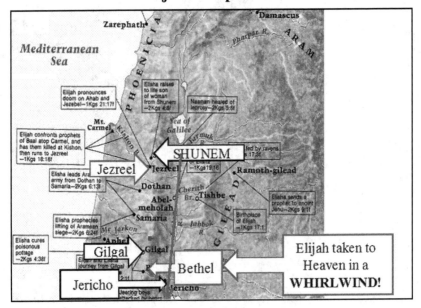

King Joram's Israel

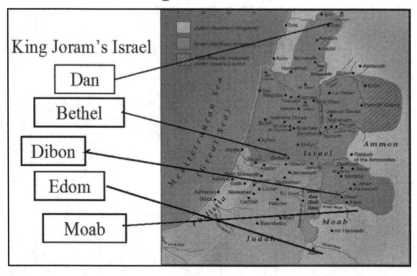

King Joram's Israel
- Dan
- Bethel
- Dibon
- Edom
- Moab

Route of Invasion

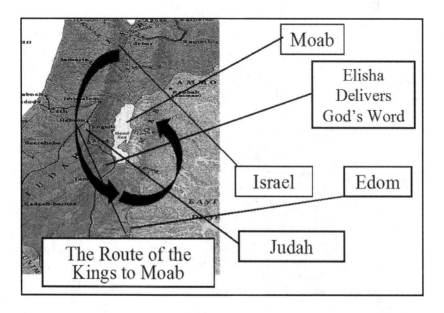

- Moab
- Elisha Delivers God's Word
- Israel
- Edom
- Judah
- The Route of the Kings to Moab

Moab to Gilgal

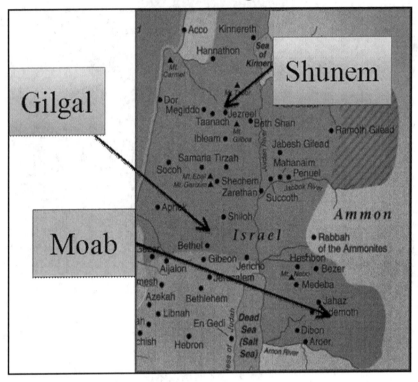

Geography

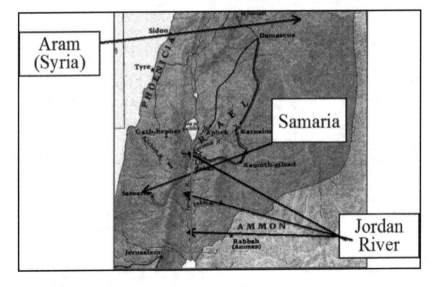

Enemy Logistical Moves

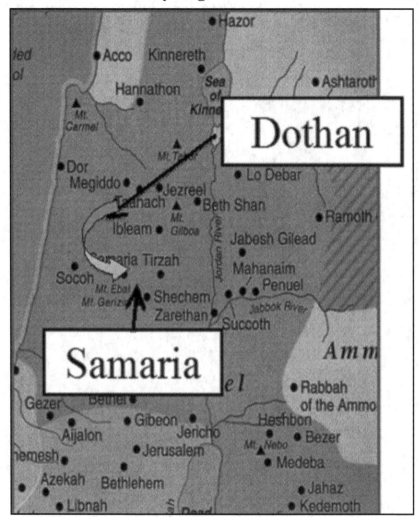

Background

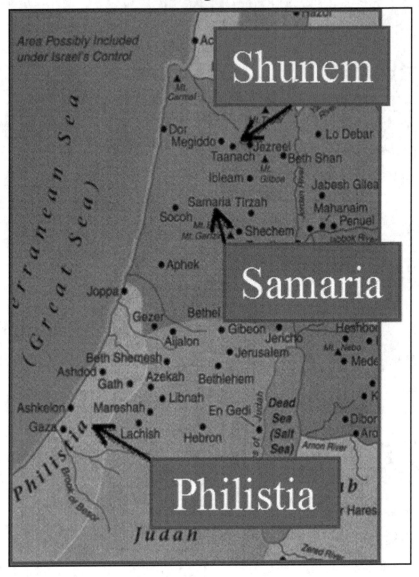

Providence of God

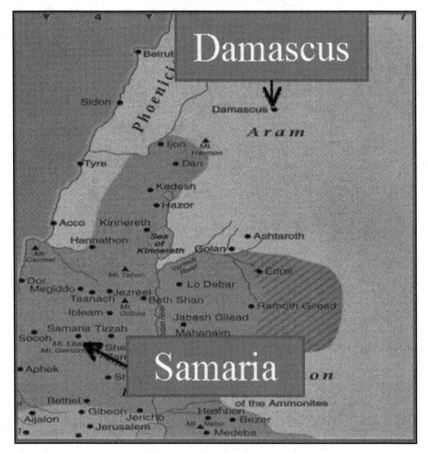

Fulfilling the Word of God

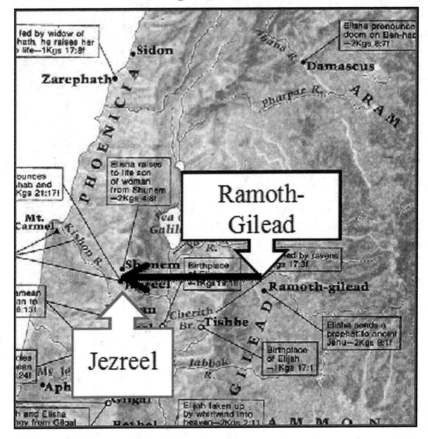

Table of Contents

Lesson 1

Finding That The Word of
Our God is Dependable

I Kings 17:1-24

Elijah is one of the great prophets of the Bible, for as Matthew Henry described it years ago,

> Never was Israel so blessed with a good prophet as it was plagued with [such] a bad king. Never was a king so bold to sin as [King] Ahab; never was a prophet so bold as to reprove and threaten [his king and people] as Elijah.... He only, of all the prophets, had the honor of Enoch, the first prophet, to be translated [to heaven], that he [too] should not see death, and the honor of Moses, [another] great prophet, to attend our Savior in his transfiguration [Matt. 17:1-13] ... Other prophets prophesied and wrote, he prophesied and acted, but he wrote nothing; but his action cast more luster on his name than their writings did on theirs. (Commentary on the Whole Bible, *Grand Rapids: Zondervan 1961, p. 385)*

Fifty-eight years had passed since the kingdom was divided after Solomon's death in 931 B.C.E. Now in 873 B.C.E., the northern ten tribes (Israel), with their capital in Samaria, had already had no less than seven kings, all of them were wicked:

1. King Jeroboam reigned for twenty-two years and was known chiefly for the two calves he made for Israel to worship in the cities of Bethel and Dan as he also installed his rival own priesthood (1 Kings 12:28-33) in the northern ten tribes of Israel.
2. King Nadab reigned over Israel for two years, but he walked in the sin of his father (1 Kings 15:26).
3. King Baasha, who took office by murdering King Nadab and Jeroboam's whole family (1 Kings 15:27-29), reigned in Israel for twenty-four years (1 Kings 15:33).
4. King Elah reigned for two years as both a drunkard and a murderer (1 Kings 16:8-9). Zimri killed him.
5. King Zimri only reigned for seven days and was found guilty of treason (1 Kings 16:15-20). He died in the fire he set in the palace to avoid the siege he was under by his own people.
6. King Omri, a military adventurer who "sinned more than all those who were before him" (1 Kings 16:25-26), reigned for twelve years.

King Ahab then took the throne and reigned for twenty-two years, but he exceeded the evil that his father Omri did. He is especially known for the fact that he married Jezebel, the daughter of the King of Sidon, a Baal worshiper (1 Kings 16:29-33). In fact, 1 Kings 16:33 reported that "Ahab also made an Asherah pole, and did more to provoke the LORD, the God of Israel, to anger than did all the kings of Israel before him." All of this was in defiance of the Lord God and plain effrontery to God.

Elijah was raised up by God to be a prophet to the people of Israel at this same time when unrighteousness was at an all-time high. He was just a simple mortal who loved God more than he loved his own life. His confrontation with the royal couple of Ahab and Jezebel was an encounter that would be worthy of prime time television in our day. He did not mince his words nor did he take time to put a nice sounding spin on his message from God. He was clearly not "politically correct."

Elijah's name meant "My God is ADONAI," which by itself stated as succinctly as possible the theme of his ministry. In his day of easy tolerance of evil and open assimilation of Canaanite religion, Elijah brought a message that pointed to the realities of the first commandment. The core of his message is found in 2 Kings 2:14b, "Where now is the LORD, the God of Elijah?" Let us now look at the beginning of his ministry in 1 Kings 17.

Text: 1 Kings 17:1-24

Title Or Subject: "Finding That The Word Of Our God Is Dependable"

Focal Point – V 24, "Now I know that you are a man of God and that the word of the LORD from your mouth is the truth."

Homiletical Keyword: Situations

Interrogative: When? (are the situations or occasions where we will find that our God's word is dependable and completely trustworthy?)

Memory Verse: (V 24 . See Above Focal Point)

The Outline

   I.   When We Abandon Our God – 17:1

   II. When We Don't Deserve God's Ministers – 17:2-7

   III. When We Come To The End Of Our Resources – 17:8-16

   IV. When We Have Given Up All Hope – 17:17-23

When We Abandon Our God – 17:1

God Brings a Special Man

While the northern ten tribes of Israel were abandoning ADONAI their God and replacing him with the worship of the Canaanite god Baal, one man, Elijah, was called by God to call this same people back to the Lord. The text begins with a suddenness and without any sort of formal introduction of this prophet, for it merely says, "Now Elijah" (1a). It is almost as sudden as when Matthew 3:1 introduced another spokesman for the Lord by saying: "In those days John the Immerser came, preaching in the Desert of Judea…"

Elijah came from Gilead, which means "hill of witness" (1a), a place that was often rocky, hard, an austere land with a jagged landscape which offered little shelter from the sun. Gilead was east of the Jordan River so Elijah had to cross it to get to Ahab's palace in northern Israel.

God Reminds Them (and Us) of a Special Relationship

In this critical hour for the nation, its king, and the people who had been called by God, a man was raised up by God to call a sinful people back to himself. This man who must have appeared to many as a country bumpkin, went directly into the palace of King Ahab and Queen Jezebel and abruptly announced his message: "As the LORD, the God of Israel lives, whom I serve, there will be neither dew nor rain in the next few years except at my word" (1b). That was it, short and not so sweet, for famines were no laughing matter in that day or in ours.

There were three important points to Elijah's announcement: (1) God was the living God, not like the dead and inert idols made of wood, stone and metal; (2) Elijah was conscious of standing, not just in the presence of human royalty, but as the phrase rendered "whom I serve" could be better translated as "in whose presence [i.e., God's] I stand;" and (3) in accordance with what God had warned in Moses' day (Deut. 11:16-17; Deut. 26 and Deut. 28),

God would remove some of the natural weather events in life, such as dew and rain, until the people came to their senses and turned back to him.

Each of these points were challenges to the king and his people. God was indeed alive and as real as any of them were. The phrase "the Living God" appears 14 times in the Tanakh and 14 times in the New Testament. Moreover, God was so real to Elijah that he was more conscious of standing in the presence of God than he was overwhelmed by being in the royal court of the Israelite king. As 2 Corinthians 5:10 said, "We must all appear before the judgment seat of Messiah to give an account of the deeds done in the body," thus Elijah felt he was always under the watchful eye of God in all that he did on earth. The third point was even more vivid, for in an agricultural economy, what would they do when there was no moisture for growing their crops. It turned out to be three and a half years in a row? But God had warned them long ago that when the people became tone deaf to his spoken word, he would speak to them through the events of history and nature in order to call them back to himself (Deuteronomy 26 and Deuteronomy 28).

Whether this was the totality of Elijah's ministry or not, we do not know, but once he was finished delivering his message from God, he turned and left the palace. It was now up to the king, queen and people to respond to God's call to them.

When We Do Not Deserve God's Ministers – 17:2-7

God Directs His Servants to Leave the Public Scene for a Time

Our Lord may at times direct his messengers to leave the public scene when the people do not deserve to hear the message of God. For example, God had sent Eli into seclusion in order to make the word of God scarce (1 Sam. 3:1). Other messengers of the Lord in our day have been called home to be with the Lord. Often, God also allows days of retirement for his servant before the next great offensive would come, for that is what happened in the case of Joseph's thirteen years in prison in Egypt, or the eighty years of Moses' learning-curve in the courts of Egypt, and the years David spent as a shepherd of the flock for his father. To this list we could also add the years Paul spent in the desert after his conversion and the days of Yeshua on earth before his last three years with his disciples. God hides his servants not to protect them but rather to make his word scarce for those who had treated it so lightly, disregarding it.

God Makes His Word Scarce

God ordered Elijah to "Leave here [Israel], turn eastward and hide in the Kerith Ravine" (3a). Elijah was not commanded to hide for his protection, but in order to prevent men and women from having a wasted experience of hearing the word of God. Often God deprived his people of the joy of hearing his word as an alarm to the semi-righteous, as Isaiah 30:20 warned: "Although the LORD gives the bread of adversity and the water of affliction, your teachers will be hidden no more, and with your own eyes you will see them." The same warning was given in Amos 8:11, "'The days are coming,' declares the Sovereign LORD, 'when I will send a famine through the land – not a famine of food or a thirst for water, but a famine of hearing the words of the LORD.'" God did this as a warning that judgment was not far away; it was time to wake up and smell the coffee!

During those days when Elijah was at the Kerith Ravine, he drank from the brook Kerith (5) and was fed by the food that the ravens brought to him (6). But why did God send him to Kerith Ravine? It was simply because that was the place where there still was a little bit of water flowing. Well then, why did God use such birds as ravens? Were they not declared in Deuteronomy 11:15 to be unclean and not to be eaten? But Elijah was not told to eat the ravens; they simply served as waiters on Elijah. Perhaps that is why they were dressed in dark black suits! Elijah could have said all of this was "for the birds," but I am sure he was glad to be fed! If you ask, what kind of food did the ravens bring? Was it just "road-kill"? Don't ask, but like Elijah be thankful for God's provision and cook it well. Why did God not use angels as his waiters on Elijah as he later will in 1 Kings 19:5? Or, why did he not use Ahab's Secretary of State, Obadiah, who fed 100 prophets of ADONAI in two caves? (1 Kings 18:4). All of these questions can be answered by the fact that God had a special lesson he wanted Elijah to learn: that he was in full control of all matters including nature itself!

God Tests His Messenger

Verse 7 went on to note that "Some time later the brook [Kerith] dried up because there had been no rain in the land." God allowed his servant Elijah to experience in part what the people he had prophesied to were now to experience. As long as there was work for Elijah to do in the service of God, he would be provided for and sustained until the Lord transported him to glory.

When We Come to The End of Our Resources – 17:8-16

God Provides From Unexpected Places

Once again God's word came to Elijah (8) as he was instructed to leave Kerith Brook and "Go at once to Zarephath of Sidon and stay there. I have commanded a widow in that place to supply you with food" (9). This must have seemed like a very strange command for the prophet, for Sidon was the place from which Queen Jezebel had come (I Kings 16:31), and where her father was king. So why would God order him to go live among a Gentile people. Were there not some rich people in Israel who could just as well maintain him during this time of famine? Later on, Yeshua raised the same question in Luke (4:25-26), but Matthew Henry captured the answer best when he said:

> To show Jezebel the impotency of her malice, God will find a
> hiding place for his servant in her [own] country.

Talk about ironies; staying in Phoenicia while Ahab and Jezebel searched the countryside for him must have set off a good laugh. So off went the prophet to what could be called "Baalsville," Phoenicia, near Sidon!

However, this is but another hint in the Tanakh that God's plan of salvation would include the Gentiles as well. God had told Abraham that in his seed, all the nations of the earth would be blessed (Gen. 12:3), which Paul identified as being in itself nothing less than the Gospel message (Gal. 3:8). Now the prophet had only an audience of two: this widow and her son!

God Provides Through Unexpected People

Elijah went without any discussion immediately to Zarephath, where he met a widow at the town gate. The Hebrew word for "widow" and the Hebrew word for "sustain" sound very much alike in Hebrew, so together they may have formed an oxymoron, another irony in the text!

Not only was his new benefactor to be a widow, but she obviously was also a Gentile, a Phoenician from Sidon, yet one who was kind-hearted and benevolent. But she had greater needs than relief from the prolonged famine that was now underway. She needed to know of the same Messiah that Israel was hearing about.

God Provides in Unexpected Ways

As Elijah arrived, the widow woman was at the city gate gathering sticks when Elijah approached her and asked, "Would you [please] bring me a little water in a jar so that I may have a drink?" (10b). Surprisingly, she turned and went immediately to get what he asked for as he called after her, "And bring me, please, a piece of bread" [or did he say a "cookie?] (11). But what was so strange about this whole encounter was that here was a Jewish man speaking to a Gentile woman on foreign soil and asking for the precious commodity of the day. Men did not speak to women, especially foreign women, and she turned out to be a widow who was down to her last drops of oil in her jug and a handful of flour in her jar (12).

She answered Elijah's request by saying, "As surely as the LORD your God lives, I don't have any bread – only a handful of flour in a jar and a little oil in a jug. I am gathering a few sticks to take home and make a meal for myself and my son that we may eat it – and die." (12) This woman knew that ADONAI [LORD] was the God in Israel, yet she too, like the Samaritan woman who talked with the Yeshua, had to know the humbling truth that "Salvation is from the Jews" (John 4:22). She knew better than to argue for supersessionism, or what is also called today Replacement Theology, wherein the Gentile believers take over all the blessings originally offered to Israel. God's promise of salvation would always come through the Messiah born in the line of Abraham, Isaac, Jacob, and David,

Elijah responded back to her dire situation with these words of hope: "Don't be afraid. Go home and do as you have said. But first make a small cake of bread for me from what you have and bring it to me, and then make something for yourself and your son." (13). Elijah even dared to say in v 14, "For this is what the LORD [ADONAI], the God of Israel says, 'The jar of flour will not be used up and the jug of oil will not run dry until the day the LORD gives rain on the land.' " God promised a miracle of multiplication if this widow woman would believe and trust him to do so. Here faith would triumph over all natural forces and objections. That is how the Psalmist put it: "O fear the LORD, you his saints, for those who fear him will lack nothing!" (Ps. 34:9). Again the palmist promised that "No good thing does [the Lord] withhold from those whose walk is blameless" (Ps. 84:11). But notice, he dared to use the "I" word up north in Gentile Phoenicia, "Israel" and her Lord God, ADONAI! That took boldness and courage!

Despite some of the crises we may face from time to time, rarely are our circumstances as desperate as those this widow and her son faced at that moment, yet we too are called to act on the same promises of God. The oil mentioned here to make the cakes is not an emblem, or a type of the Holy Spirit, as some may want to say, but it is a symbol of the powerful presence of the Living God. When God delivers his mighty word, it does not come back to us empty and void of any real effectiveness; it does what it was sent to do! (Isa. 55).

When We Abandon All Hope – 17:17-24

God Is Wise in What He Allows

Verse 17 is best translated as "After these thing," i.e., the miraculous signs of the multiplication of the oil and flour, that the widow's son suddenly became ill, and then he stopped breathing, which is usually a very serious condition (17b). When that happened, all of a sudden the woman who had lost her husband sometime in the past, and was now about to lose her son, turned on the prophet and must have yelled, "What do you have against me, man of God? Did you come to remind me of my sin and kill my son?" (18). Does this mean we must pay for our blessings? After all, hadn't she just seen the miracle of the daily multiplication of the oil and flour! Not at all, for there is no merit or working for the blessing of God, so what was bothering this woman? Was there some hidden sin she had never faced before the Lord and now she figured that this prophet had brought it to light? What poor theology she had!

Elijah did not yell back at her and complain that he too was sick and tired of being pent-up in this house with this woman and her son. He did not say that as a prophet he was used to being out around the masses of people, proclaiming the word of the Lord. No! Instead, he simply stretched out his arms and said, "Give me your son" (19). It is a wonder that this woman did not absolutely refuse and say, "No! He's all that I have; I have lost everything else in this world and you can't have his corpse!" But she was too weak to argue anymore; life had been very hard on her. She let Elijah take her son in his arms and go outside to ascend the stairs to his prophet's chamber, a room on the flat roof.

Elijah laid the boy on his bed as he cried out to the Lord, "O LORD my God, have you brought tragedy also upon this widow I am staying with, by causing her son to die? (20). Some of us would want to hush Elijah up a bit, for he now appears to accuse God of introducing added tragedy beside the famine that had by now affected many middle eastern countries. The prophet stretched himself out over the boy three times and prayed: "Let this boy's life return to him." (21b).

God Is Mighty in What He Does

The Lord heard Elijah's cry (22a). When God hears, he both hears and acts as part of the same "hearing," for it is not as we say when we answer our phones with "Hello, this is he." But, when God hears, the text said: "And the boy's life returned to him and he lived" (22b). Elijah picked up the boy and took him down the stairs from his rooftop room and gave him back to his mother alive. He exclaimed: "Look, your son is alive." (23b). Can you imagine the surprise and joy in that household?

Now it was the widow woman's turn to speak, for all of a sudden a lot of things became clear for her. She said, "Now I know that you are a man of God and that the word of the LORD from your mouth is the truth" (24). She must have smacked her forehead as she said that—Now I know! Yes, "The eyes of the Lord are on the righteous and his ears are attentive to their prayers" (1 Pet. 3:12). This woman learned what we need to learn: we can depend on the word of God, for it is absolutely dependable and truthful in all that it teaches.

Conclusions

1. If it is asked, as the theme of this section does ask: "Where is the LORD God of Elijah?" the answer can be found in the testimony of this widow woman and all who have cried out to the Lord. He can be seen in his word and in his mighty works of miracles!

2. God's word is still on the "cutting edge," especially in these troubled times today.
3. One calledman or one called-woman plus God still equals a majority!
4. Are not the natural disasters an opportunity to listen for the call of God for repentance while there is hope for God's deliverance and our survival?

Questions for Thought and Reflection

1. What counts in life in the long-run? Is it wealth? Knowledge? Or the fear of God?
2. If God has proven himself true in the judgments he said he would send on mortals, and they have occurred, can we not count on him to be true in the blessings and encouraging forecasts he has given for the future?
3. What sorts of obstacles, problems, issues, or questions, that I may have, can compare to the power, presence and veracity of the Living God?

Lesson 2

Experiencing a God Who Answers Prayer by Fire

1 Kings 18:1-32

"If there is a God, I wish he would prove it to me, because I haven't seen any evidence of his existence or his work," say some often with a pugnacious attitude. And that is what the prophet Elijah was dealing with in these hardened idolaters in Israel. "If God were alive and real, we could not all have gone so quickly for all that Baal stuff, they quipped; we would have stayed close to the Lord." Meanwhile, a Gentile foreigner, the widow woman Elijah was staying with was slowly coming to the reality that Elijah's God was the real God: he was able to multiply the flour and oil and he was able to raise the dead and bring them back to life again: surely that meant he was the real God! She had never seen any of the idols of wood and stone do any of those things! People usually stay dead once they die!

But now, at last, the forced seclusion and isolation of Elijah was about to come to an end and he was about to demonstrate to the vacillating people of Israel a most spectacular live public demonstration that the Canaanite prophets were phonies and ADONAI alone was God of gods, Lord of lords! Thus, to get things started, the Lord instructed Elijah, "after many days, …. in the third year," to go and present himself to King Ahab. If Elijah

were to go to Ahab, then the Lord would send rain on the land"
(18:1). Now this was a real risky move for God's prophet, for the
king and especially the queen must have been mad as hops at this
backwoodsman, whom they regarded as some kind of country
buffoon. If only they could get their hands on him, they would
show him a thing or two! Who gave him the right to turn off the
rain and dew anyway! But Elijah went to meet the king without
complaint or protest; he would confront this unhappy king, for God
would be with him and help him. Therefore, Elijah obeyed, for the
famine had long since reached a state of being "severe in Samaria"
(2). Once again, the prophet trekked back from Zarephath through
his own homeland to carry out his mission from God. Surely he
saw along the way how the green pastures had turned into dry
stubble and parched fields with skeletal remains of both wild and
domestic animals scattered everywhere. No doubt there were
stiffened corpses of the poor and destitute people also along the
roads, which he could see, especially as he got close to villages
and towns where men and women and children had collapsed
in their tracks from hunger and thirst. There was no water to be
observed anywhere and no babbling streams and brooks to fill the
air with their music; it was like a scene out of a horror movie in
which there was only death, decay, rot, and evidence of God's
judgment all over the hills and valleys. Disobedience to the Lord
is costly and comes with a high price!

Now King Ahab had commanded Obadiah, his sort of chief of
staff in the palace (perhaps like a Secretary of State), to join him in
a search of all the land of Israel to see if there was any grass left in
any spot so they could keep the horses and mules alive; how could
the government have a parade without these animals! Obadiah
was to go one way and Ahab would go the other way in search of
grass: the parade horses (perhaps they were Clydesdales) had to
kept alive at all costs; never mind the people! There, friends, was
a leader with a real heart that wanted to serve his people (i.e., once
the horses and the mules were fed)!

Obadiah, as it turns out, was a true believer in ADONAI. This could be seen in the fact that while Jezebel was killing off the Lord's prophets, Obadiah had secreted away in two caves 100 ADONAI prophets and provided for them each day with food and water (4). So as Obadiah was walking along in search of any green grass, suddenly Elijah pops up right in front of him! (7a) Obadiah could not believe his eyes; he yelled: "Is it really you, my lord Elijah?" (7b). "Yes," responded Elijah. "Go tell your master, 'Elijah is here'" (8). But that sounded like a death-trap to Obadiah, for he complained, "You are handing your servant over to Ahab to put me to death" (9). Obadiah went on, you know my master has looked all over the whole countryside for you and he has even made nations take an oath that they too could not find you. So if I go and say I just met you, and you suddenly disappear, what will I do then? I don't know if the Spirit of the LORD might pick you up and remove you so that I will be left holding the bag (10-12). I assure you, Elijah, that I am a real Kosher believer in ADONAI, for you must have heard somewhere that I am taking care of 100 hidden ADONAI prophets each day (13-14).

To all of this Elijah simply said: "As the LORD Almighty lives, whom I serve, I will surely present myself to Ahab today" (15). With that assurance, off Obadiah went with the startling discovery and news for Ahab (16).

When Ahab finally arrived and faced Elijah, the best he could manage to say was: "Is that you, you troubler of Israel? (17). Not so, responded Elijah, but I will tell who has made trouble for Israel: It's you and your family; you have disregarded the commands God has given to us and you all have followed the Baals (18). So if you want to see rain again, you had better summon the people from all ten tribes to meet me on Mount Carmel. Yes, bring those 450 prophets of Baal and the 400 prophets of Asherah (19), who eat at Jezebel's table (apparently paid for with tithes of the people to ADONAI). What could Ahab do? He had run out of all his options; he was utterly helpless in the face of the nation torn apart by famine and thirst. So Ahab sent out word and assembled the people and false prophets on Mount Carmel as he had been instructed.

Elijah was now in charge; not the king or queen! She must have been so mad at Elijah that she did not even attend the event! As Elijah stood before the people, he asked this question" "How long will you waver/sit one the fence between two opinions? If the LORD/Adonai is God follow him; but if Baal is god, follow him" (21). The people "said nothing" (21c). Of course not: what was there to say? They were all dying. It was A W. Pink who commented on the people's silence by saying:

> O for that plain and faithful preaching which would reveal to men the unreasonableness of their position … that every objection would be silenced and they would stand self-condemned.[1]

The word to "waver" can also be rendered to "totter," or to "halt," which meant that the people were limping and not walking uprightly. Instead, they were like intoxicated persons who were all over the place in their allegiance to the Lord; fickle, inconstant, eclectic, syncretistic, pluralistic and lukewarm in their devotion to their Lord. Elijah's summons was much like Moses' at the Golden Calf: "Who is one the Lord's side? Let him come to me. (Exod 32:26). Yeshua also said: "He that is not with me is against me" (Matt. 12:30). It was time for Israel to declare its allegiance, one way or the other; God would not take any second place arrangement in anyone's heart.

It was time for the final showdown between Adonai and Baal to begin; it was decided that the four hundred and fifty prophets would go first in calling down fire (22). They were to get two bulls, one of themselves and one for Elijah. Their bull they were to dissect on the altar on top of the wood, but they were not to set fire to the wood. It was time for them to go ahead and show the perhaps two million persons gathered on Mount Carmel what sort

---

[1]   A. W. Pink, *The Life of Elijah*, London, The Banner of Truth Trust, 1956, 1963, p 127.

of stuff Baal is made of: "Call on him as best you can, and ask him to set the sacrifice on fire," Elijah urged in an unbelieving voice and attitude, "for the God who answers by fire, he is God" (23-24). This was all agreed to by Elijah and the Baal prophets (24c). So they called with all their might! They continued to cry out balefully, but there was no response; no one answered; no one paid attention; there was not even a little bit of smoke! This was turning out to be a real embarrassment; too bad Jezebel was not here to cheer on her students. Perhaps she knew the real key to getting Baal to answer; instead she was back at the Summer palace residence in Jezreel, stewing over that vagabond Elijah and the grief he had brought into her nice plans for Israel. Did she have a hunch that things might not go well for her Baal prophets? Is that why she declined to attend such an important national contest?

But enough was enough; at least for Elijah. It now 3:00 p.m. and the Baal shenanigans had gone on for nine hours. Certainly that was more than enough time to rouse a most reluctant deity no matter how busy he might have been. But over across the miles from Mount Carmel in Jerusalem, it was time for the evening sacrifice to be offered as usual, so Elijah said, "Repair the mess these guys have made of this sacrificial site: It's my turn to call down fire."

Elijah began by calling the people to gather in closer to him as the repairs to the busted up altar were going on (30). The shenanigans of Baal prophets with the bruises and cuts they inflicted on themselves and each other with their swords and spears must have driven the people to retreat at a distance, maybe to protect their children from watching up c lose this gross display of foolishness. Elijah repaired the torn down altar by selecting twelve stones to rebuild the altar – one stone for each tribe in Israel. Now there was an act that was not politically correct; after all, he was in northern Yankee territory; Israel had broken away from the two southern tribes of Judah and Benjamin. But Elijah recalled for them how they got their name of Israel, for the Lord had used

those very same words: "Your name shall be Israel," when Jacob
had wrestled the angel of the Lord at Peniel (Gen. 32:28) and again
when Jacob ordered his family to get rid of their foreign gods as
they buried them under the Oak tree in Shechem (Gen. 35:10). If
those had been occasions for revival, then it was revival time once
again on Mount Carmel. Elijah continued his preparation of the
altar by digging a trench around its base deep enough to hold 24
pounds of seed. He then dissected the bull and laid it on the wood.
However, he still needed on more action before all was ready. He
ordered some men to go down the mountain side to the waters
of the Mediterranean Sea and fill four large jars with water. This
water was to be poured over the offering and the wood. They were
to do this, not just once, they were to make the trip up and down
the mountain three times and to pour the water on the offering and
wood until everything was soaking wet and the freshly dug trench
was filled with water. Now everything was set.

Can't you just hear the whispering of the crowd: "I don't see
how anything is going to light that fire; it's too wet!" "This will
never work!" "Who does this Elijah think he is? Is he some kind of
wonder-worker?" "I don't think the Baal guys or this Elijah dude
will able to pull this off; no one has ever taken on this type of bet
before?" "I don't think this will get us anywhere; we should all
just live and let live is what I say."

It was now time for Elijah to step forward and announce what
he was going to do, which he did in a way; however he just prayed
to God! It was not a long drawn out prayer, with him peeking out
of one eye to see if there was any smoke yet. Nor did he try to
stonewall his guests or God by extending his prayer to include the
missionaries to gain more time or the like. No, he went straight to
the heart of the matter and in some 60 Hebrew words or less he
prayed:

> LORD, the God of Abraham, Isaac, and Israel, let it be known
> today that you are God in Israel and that I am your servant
> and have done all these things at your command. Answer me,

LORD, answer me, so that these people will know that you, LORD, are God, and that you are turning their hearts back again [to yourself]. (1 Kings 18:36-37).

God's answer came immediately, for "Then the fire of the LORD fell and burned up the sacrifice, the wood, the stones and the soil, and also licked up the water in the trench" (38). That must have been overwhelming and convincing for even any atheists who might have been present. Too bad, Jezebel missed these fireworks.

The people were just blown away by the obvious demonstration of the power of God. I wonder what the 850 prophets of Baal and Asherah thought about all of this? Had they made a huge mistake in trying to syncretistically worship ADONAI and Baal? The vast majority of the people, however, fell face down and cried out: "The LORD - he is God! The LORD – he is God! (39). Were the majority of those attending that day sincere in their affirmation or was it simply an emotion that came from the pressure of the moment? We do not know for sure. Also, had the widow woman, with whom Elijah had stayed, slipped in among that Jewish crowd to see Elijah's public display of the work of God as she had seen the Work God had done for her in her home? Again, there is no evidence to suggest she did or did not attend the Mount Carmel display of the power of God.

But another question arises: Why had God used the sign of "fire" as evidence of his presence when what was so badly needed was rain? The Lord had sent fire on other occasions; for example when the Tabernacle was dedicated (Deut. 9:24), when the land David bought from Araunah for an altar on what would become the Temple platform (1 Chron. 21:26), and when Solomon's Temple was dedicated (2 Chron. 7:1). God had indicated his presence and approval by sending down fire from heaven. What was the significance of the fire, then?

In this case on Mount Carmel, it was the theology of a substitute in the sacrifice offered to the Lord. Before the blessings of the rain could come, a substitute had to intervene. The fire also symbolized the revelation of the divine name as it had at the burning in Moses' day (Exod 3:15). God was there present on Mount Carmel with his servant Elijah. By these means the people of Israel would come to know that the Lord alone was God and that he it was who was at that moment turning their hearts back to himself to serve him. Despite all of the hobgoblin prancing around the altar by the masochistic wielding prophet-priests of Baal in hopes that their own spilled blood would compel their deity to respond to them, they came up empty and devoid of any answer from him.

When the fire of God fell, it was no natural flash of lightning; it was the supernatural intervention by the Lord himself as could be seen in the fact that it consumed no only the pieces of the bull on the altar and the wood underneath it, but it also devoured the stones and the water in the trench surrounding the altar. No wonder all the people immediately fell down and worshiped the Lord.

Elijah Prays For Rain – 1 Kings 18:41-46.

Elijah prayed not only in public out on the mountain side that the Lord would make himself known to Israel, but now he prays in private that God would send the rain. Some will wonder, why should he pray? Hadn't God already promised that if Elijah would go and meet Ahab that the rain would come (18:1)? Thus we learn that the promises of God were not meant to deter us from praying specifically, but instead these promises were meant to teach us what it was that we should pray for!

However, there is more to learn from Elijah's example of prayer. First of all he withdrew from the crowd and went to the top of Mount Carmel where he could be alone with God (42b). Then this prophet prostrated himself by bending down to the ground as he put his face between his knees (42c). As he prayed, he instructed his servant to go and look out over the Mediterranean Sea to tell him if he saw any signs of the coming rain (43a). But time after time, the servant reported there was nothing to match what the prophet was hoping for (43b). In the meantime, Elijah remained fervent in prayer while continuing to be watchful and fully expectant of God's rainstorm that would begin soon. There was no doubt that Elijah's prayer was also definite just as Zechariah 10:1 had instructed. It was as James 5:16 had promised: "The prayer worked-in [by the Holy Spirit] is effective" (My translation). Thus it was on the seventh trip to survey the western skies over the Mediterranean Sea that Elijah's servant reported the good news that he had seen "a cloud as small as a man's hand rising from the sea" (44). That was what Elijah had sought God in prayer, so he told his servant: "Go tell Ahab, 'Hitch up your chariot and go down before the rain stops you" (44b). Meanwhile, the "sky grew black with clouds, the wind rose, a heavy rain started falling and Ahab rode off to Jezreel" (45). Simultaneously with all this going on, "The power of the LORD came on Elijah and, tucking his cloak into his belt, he ran ahead of Ahab all the way to Jezreel" (46) – distance of some 18 miles! Elijah did this not to prove his athleticism, or to bring him to his summer palace unharmed, but as an indication of the continuing power of God with his prophet who would stand in that same power to assist Ahab if he would turn back to ADONAI.

But some ask: What became of the 850 prophets? Elijah had commanded that all of them were to be seized so that not one escaped. Furthermore, they were to be brought off the mountain down to the Kishon Valley where Elijah had them slaughtered (40). To our modern ears, that sounds awful; but one had to realize the damage these frauds were for so many who had already passed out of this life previously believing that they could go to be with ADONAI in eternity by splitting their vote: half for Baal and half for ADONAI. But God will not compete with any other God; a person must be all for the Lord or not at all. A person who was half for the Lord was altogether against him

Conclusions

1. Our Lord has always had his special servants like Elijah who served him without display or public affirmation.
2. After Israel had suffered for three and a half years, the Lord said it was time to show his presence, his power and his glory to the nation. They had to see that the drought and famine were not merely the result of some bad luck; instead it was as a result of his trying to get the nation's attention and repentance.
3. Leaders can be the real troublers of God's people when they try to lead without placing him first in their lives.
4. There are times when God says it is time to choose whom it is that we will serve: will it be another god or will it be ADONAI?
5. When the fire of God fell on Elijah's sacrifice, it was clear that the power of God was without any competition or imitation.
6. The school of prayer takes time and it takes paying attention to what God has declared and taught in his word.
7. There are times when evil must be thoroughly liquidated because the perpetrators of the evil have had more than enough time to go back and retrace the wicked path they had wrongly chosen many years ago.

Questions for Discussion and Reflection

1. Is there ever any connection between the disasters in a nation and the weather with the warnings that God has given to the peoples of the earth in his word?
2. Is it possible to serve as leaders in the halls of government when they may not be committed to the principles of the word of God?
3. How could Elijah be so sure that God would answer his prayer for fire to come down from heaven in the face of several million people present, when he had never tried this before?
4. The prophets of false religion are oftentimes embarrassed by their inability to compete with the overriding power of the hand of God. Does this cause them to see the difference and to come to God for salvation?

Lesson 3

Fits of Depression
Versus a New Vision of God

1 Kings 19:1-21

Elijah had raced on foot ahead of King Ahab's royal chariot entourage as it left Mount Carmel, which now in 1 Kings 19 was arriving at Ahab and Jezebel's palace in Jezreel, 18 miles southeast from Mount Carmel - a good distance, but short of a full marathon run. Perhaps the prophet and the king were by now soaked to their skin from the downpour as Ahab went into the palace to report to Jezebel what had happened that day on Mount Carmel. But Elijah surely was left outside with the rain water still dripping from the prophet's sweaty beard, as he no doubt tried to get out from being under the downpour, and so he stood there waiting to see what was going to happen when Ahab told his wife the news. It had been a most thrilling day, for God had dramatically answered his prayer for fire to fall from heaven; the prophets of Baal, however, had suffered a resounding defeat and Israel was now relieved of perhaps all 850 no-good prophets of Baal and Asherah. Perhaps, hoped Elijah, the long anticipated spiritual revival had now arrived in Israel, wherein the palace, the populace, and the press all would immediately come to the Lord with genuine repentance and turn back to the God of their fathers. Of course, Elijah was exhausted from such an exhilarating day, but he could not have been more elated over what God had done. God had so dramatically and definitely answered his prayer that surely things would really turn around in the nation to the praise, honor, and glory of the name of ADONAI after they had witnessed the marvel of the heaven-sent fire. Perhaps the prophet could now act now act as a spiritual counselor for King Ahab, just as King David had found Nathan the prophet to serve his government. But how would Jezebel react to the bad news she was now hearing? There was no telling what she might do once she found out what had happened to her seminary of idol worshippers. She could really get uncontrollably mad!

The Wrath of Jezebel

As Elijah no doubt waited outside, where it was raining, to be invited inside the palace, Ahab was in the meantime giving to his wife the news of what had taken place that day, for Jezebel apparently had refused to attend this contest. Did she have a hunch that her prophets were all trained frauds? Anyway, it had not gone well for her prophets, her husband informed her; in fact, they had not been able to produce one drop of any water, or even a smidgen of smoke, much less the required fire falling from heaven, according to the rules of the contest! Her prophets had lost face with the people badly that very day! What's more, Elijah had slaughtered her whole retinue of prophets, so she was now technically owner of a non-prophet organization (sorry about the pun!). When she heard of this slaughter of her inept students, she really got steamed; she let go a stream of curses against this prophet of ADONAI. One in particular grabbed Elijah's attention, for she had send a messenger outside to make sure Elijah heard it just as she had uttered it:

> May the gods deal with me, be it ever so severely, if by this
> time tomorrow I do not make your life like one of them [i.e.,
> like one of the slain prophets of Baal and Asherah] (19:2).

She was mad as hops! But why did she give Elijah 24 hour notice? I do not know. It may have been that she was aware of the fact that often many of us are weakest in the very area of our strengths? Jezebel attacked the courage of God's prophet! And that surely knocked Elijah off his pins, for he suddenly and uncharacteristically was terribly "afraid and ran for his life" (3). Elijah fled from Jezebel's presence? He had just finished running 18 miles from Mount Carmel, but taking off again was no problem, for he was going to get out of there as fast as his feet could take him. That woman was savage and a known killer of prophets! But why did Elijah run away from her? Hadn't he just come from calling down fire from heaven? Why didn't he rebuke her by something like this to her? "Madam Queen, do you want to become a grease spot? I have just finished working with God by calling down fire from heaven, and if you are going to act this way, the Lord and I might just have to continue doing the same thing, with you as the target, so stop threatening me! I am a true prophet of ADONAI and all Israel has borne witness to that very fact today!" That might have given that woman room for some retractions and let some of the wind out of her sails! But no; in the very area of Elijah's strength, i.e., his courage and deep dependence on God, he faltered, and instead he ran for his life out of fear of being liquidated by this savage woman!

Part of Jezebel's problem may well have been Ahab, for God's prophet Elijah had predicted a drought on the basis of the divine word that was available to the whole nation, but Ahab still didn't get it; he attributed the drought directly and personally to Elijah, not to God! Was his father King Omri so anti-God, we wonder, that Ahab had never been taken to Sunday School or the temple? God gave Ahab three and a half years during the duration of the drought for him to "get it," but never once did Ahab consider repenting of his sin, or of possibly turning his heart and life over to God; no, he was going to stonewall God and tough it out. Things would eventually get better, he hoped; they had to! Even now as the rains pounded down on the palace roof at Jezreel, Ahab focused his report to the queen on the unprecedented fact that Elijah had killed her prophets. However, the drought had been broken! Wasn't anybody thankful that the rains had finally come at long last? Wasn't anyone keeping the main thing the main thing? For Ahab and Jezebel, however, it was all about politics, the economy, and her idea of what religion was all about, but for the two of them, it was not about the theology of the living God - ADONAI!

Elijah had hit Jezebel where it hurt, for she was a real religious Baal-and-Asherah-freak, who was utterly devoted to the worship of her gods. But for Ahab, this did not seem to matter one way or the other; he was just not into this religious stuff one way or the other. As Jezebel simmered down a bit, it may have occurred to her that her antagonist was right outside, standing just out of the reach of the downpour. The thought may have occurred to her, why not send a guard out there and polish Elijah off? But if Elijah had just finished doing all this in front of a standing-room-crowd of perhaps two million people, so by now he must have been something of an instant hero and a sure worker of miracles in the minds of the people. If she killed him on her doorsteps, the people might revolt and that certainly would spark a coup against Ahab's government, so she decided to threaten him severely and then catch up with him at some other distant place where it would not look so suspicious, as if she had caused it. No sense provoking a military or popular revolt at this time! Whatever her strategy, however, it worked!

A Prophet on the Run – 19:3-14

Elijah had gone all in one day from the heights of exhilaration, blessing, and joy to the depths of despair, disappointment, and disgust. He continued running away from Jezebel some 75 miles or so south until he came to Beersheba in Judah, where he flopped down under a Broom/Juniper Bush and sobbed out this depressing prayer:

I have had enough LORD. Take my life; I am no better than my ancestors. (4).

He couldn't have been all that serious about the Lord taking his life, for if he had stayed in Jezreel, Jezebel would have taken his life free of charge! No, he had been overtaken by the blues and perhaps even now was suffering from a bad case of depression. How is it that we mortal creatures can go from such heights of blessing and fabulous joy to the pits and sloughs of despondency - all in the space of a few hours? Is not the great nineteenth century preacher, Charles Haddon Spurgeon an example of the same type of extreme shifting from the heights of joy to the bottom of the pit of despair? He wrote:

> Fits of depression come over most of us .... The strong are not always vigorous, the wise are not always courageous, and the joyous not always happy .... Such was my experience when I first became a pastor in London. My success appalled me; and the thought of the career which it seemed to open up, so far from elating me, cast me into the lowest depth ..... Who was I that I should continue to lead so great a multitude. [2]

What had come over God's prophet? Just a day or so ago he was a courageous pioneer who, along with his Lord, had faced off two million people with no hesitations at all. He had no fear of 450 prophets of Baal, or 400 prophets of Asherah, or of the vast majority of the nation that loved Baal worship. He apparently did not even worry about getting caught by Ahab's searchers who hunted for him during the three and a half years of the drought. So how was it that one woman had upset his apple-cart and turned him into a fearful fugitive? Elijah suddenly had to deal with three factors in his life: fear, a female, and flight to Sinai.

---

2 C. H. Spurgeon, "Lectures to My Students" (reprint, Grand Rapids, MI.: Associated Publishers and Authors, 1971, pp. 167, 173 as cited by Charles R. Swindoll, *The Life and Times of Elijah*, Anaheim, CA.: *Insight for Living*, 1992, p. 565.

All of these issues had arisen because he was placing his eyes on the human factors and not on the Lord. Nothing had changed from what he had faced before: there still was the opposition from the Baal cult, from Queen Jezebel, and from a nation that had forsaken ADONAI. Nor had he waited for instructions from the Lord as to what he was to do after the drought ended with the mighty downpour. Like the apostle Peter, who took his eyes off the Lord and began to sink as he tried to walk on the water of the Sea of Galilee, so was Elijah sinking as well. He needed to get his eyes back on the Lord.

There was another problem: Elijah must have feared failure, for he had hoped that one huge public demonstration of God's presence and his power would move the whole nation to change its thinking and lifestyle in favor of the Lord – especially among the royal leadership in Samaria. But no, Jezebel and Ahab apparently were totally unfazed by such overwhelming evidence for the power and presence of ADONAI. Elijah must have thought he was a real failure. Those two leaders of the nation had not repented or showed any sign of changing their allegiances from idols to being exclusively dedicated to the Living God. What had gone wrong? Had the prophet missed something he was supposed to have done? Three and a half years of waiting and praying, and yet despite one fantastic day of triumph, now it seemed as if nothing had really happened or taken place. Was nothing to come from three and a half years of waiting on the Lord? Would the nation and its leaders continue on as they had in the past?

Now, south of Beersheba in the wilderness of Negev, a real no-man's land, in what must have been scorching heat of the sun, Elijah dismissed his servant, for he apparently was resigning his office as prophet – his services were no longer required! Thus our discouraged prophet sought whatever shade he could find from some old Broom Bush as a consolation for his depressed spirits. It wasn't much shade, come to think of it, for this was no towering oak tree, it was only an old scrub bush; there he collapsed and fell into a troubled sleep (3-5a).

Our prophet felt like he was completely spent: physically he was fatigued; spiritually he had lost his bearings; emotionally he was depressed; vocationally he was now unemployed, since he had just released his servant and in effect had quit the ministry! He faced what he believed was an overwhelming physical and spiritual letdown – nothing seemed to be going right for him. What could fix these sorts of problems? Nothing seemed to help! He was a has-been!

God, however, could attend to just such blues and sloughs of despondency. He sent an angel who touched him and ordered him: "Get up and eat." There by his head was food, perhaps cooked over a hibachi stove (out in the middle of the desert mind you), and possibly a jug of cool water as well (6). Elijah ate and drank, then he lay down once again to get some more sleep. He was really exhausted! But then the Angel of the LORD, perhaps Messiah himself in a Christophany, came back a second time and once again gently touched him, repeating the same therapy he had just performed for him. Our Lord knew that "the journey [had been] quite a trip for [him]" (7c). Once again, he enjoyed a personally cooked hot meal.

"Strengthened by that food," (8a), Elijah continued on his path to the south. This was a journey that should only have taken ten days (Deut. 1:2), but Elijah must have moped along at the speed of a tortoise, for he spent 40 days and 40 nights until he arrived at "Horeb," otherwise known as Mount Sinai. When he arrived there, "he went into *the* cave and spent the night" (9). But why did the Hebrew text include an article before the word for "cave?" No cave had appeared previously in this text or in the previous narrative about Elijah, so what cave was the author referring to? It had to be the same place Moses had used when Israel had fallen into sin by constructing the Golden Calf (Exod 33:21).

After Elijah arrived at Sinai, the Lord asked him pointedly: "What are you doing here, Elijah?" (9b). Obviously, Elijah was way off base and had had no instructions from God about going to

Sinai; nor had Elijah any business resigning his post and releasing his servant. It was time for Elijah to wake up and smell the coffee. God would still use him, but there would be some missed opportunities which he otherwise might have had. He would appoint someone to take his place.

Elijah had a pat answer to God's question, "What are you doing here, Elijah?" for he no doubt had rehearsed in his mind over and over his answer to our Lord's inquiry:

> I have been very zealous for the LORD God Almighty. The Israelites have rejected your covenant, torn down your altars, and put your prophets to death with the sword. I am the only one left and now they are trying to kill me too (10).

All of this was true -- at least some of it was true of Jezebel, but this was not the time, nor the place, to debate these matters. Elijah needed most of all to get his vision clarified and he sorely needed all over again a whole new concept of the person, might, and majesty of God. That is why the Lord commanded him: "Get out and stand on the mountain in the presence of the LORD, for the LORD is about to pass by" (11).

That command must have immediately brought to Elijah's mind another moment in the past when God had told his servant Moses, who was depressed over the idolatry that his people had fallen into while he was up on Mount Sinai talking with God for forty days and forty nights. Moses had now asked the Lord to show him his "glory" (Exod 33:18). The Lord had responded by saying that he would "cause all his goodness to pass in front of [Moses], ... and [he would] proclaim [his] name" (33:19). So the Lord told Moses where to stand on a rock near him (33:21), for when he caused all his "glory to pass by," he would put Moses in "in a cleft of the rock and cover [him] with [his] hand until [he had] passed by." Then God would "remove [his] hand and [Moses would] see [God's] *back*" (33:22-23). But God is a spirit and those who worship him must worship him in spirit and truth (John 4:24).

The word translated "back" of the Lord is "the after," or "that which comes afterwards." Then our Lord saw that his glory was too brilliant for Moses, so that his face had to be shielded by God's hand, but what the Lord allowed him to see was the "after burn" of his glory. Those of us in the space age ought to be able to translate this word for what follows "after" the glow of his glory.

All too often what God's servants need in their days of deep misgivings and dejections is a whole new vision of the majesty and glory of God. Instead of reviewing our problems over and over again, we need to take one more steady and long look at our Lord and experience once again his power, his presence, his magnificence – in short, to let all his goodness pass before our memories once again. Thinking about Jezebel was no substitute for thinking about the Living God!

In John Bunyan's *The Pilgrim's Progress*, the main character is "Christian," who like Elijah falls into the "Slough of Despond." After he struggled to get out, finally "Help" comes and assists him out of the pit. When Christian asks his friend Help why this slough is here for travelers to stumble into, Help responds: "This miry slough is such a place as cannot be mended." There are such pits in the life of a Believer, but the Lord is our helper who will not only assist us in getting out, but will give us a whole new picture of himself to change us by his power and his presence and glory.

A Call to Go Back

Our Lord did not argue with Elijah, for after all, he is Lord of all. He simply said to Elijah:

> Go back the way you came, and go up to the desert of Damascus. When you get there, anoint Hazael king over Aram. Also anoint Jehu the son of Nimshi king over Israel, and anoint Elisha son of Shaphat from Abel-meholah to succeed you as prophet. Jehu will put to death any who escape the sword of Hazael, and Elisha will put to death any who escape the sword of Jehu. (1 Kings 19:15-17)

Our Lord had dealt with those of his servants who had similar experiences to Elijah before his time. Had he not had to deal with Moses when he had "spoken unadvisedly with his lips." (Ps. 106:32-33; Num 20:10)? Likewise, he had had to deal with King Saul when the prophet Samuel delayed his coming and King Saul went ahead and offered the sacrifice that the priests alone were to offer (1 Sam. 15:17-19). In the same way, the Lord had to deal with Elijah, for even though he was restored to service for the Lord once more, he never was reinstated in quite the position he had occupied before his flight to Sinai. True, God had told him to return to the place he had left, but his work now would consist of anointing three men who would now share among them the ministry that he might have fulfilled if only he had kept to the path he had been on. These words shout loudly the same teaching our Lord gave in John's gospel. There Yeshua had taught,

> I am the vine; you are the branches. If you remain in me and
> I in you, you will bear much fruit; apart from me you can do
> nothing. (John 15:5)

Elijah needed to continue abiding in the Lord; he could not do the work he was called to do by himself. If he was worried about what was going to happen to his ministry in the days after he was gone, then our Lord had a solution; he would give him a companion, Elisha who would take up the ministry where he had left off. Elijah seemed to disappear from the public scene for the next ten years and he seemed to concentrate on training in what he called his schools of the "sons of the prophets." They together would leave an indelible mark on that generation in the days ahead as those who had been trained would continue the work alongside of his new companion Elisha.

God also told Elijah that he would raise up a Syrian king named Hazael who would be the rod of divine vengeance for Israel at large (2 Kings 8:12; 10:32; 12:3, 17). Likewise, King Jehu would be the divine scourge to the house of Ahab as he ridded Israel of that dynasty, root and branch. But Elisha's ministry would go on with the favor and blessing of God. God would accomplish his work despite the failure of Elijah. Moreover, no one would escape the judgment of God; God's sieves are extremely fine and he can eventually catch all who seem to have escaped his judgments, for the one avoiding and seemingly escaping the sword of Hazael will Jehu slay and the ones escaping the sword of Jehu will Elisha slay. God's nets will eventually catch up with all those who oppose him and refuse to believe in him.

Elijah had twice blurted out to the Lord that he was the solitary believer left in Israel, but he was grossly mistaken! God had some seven thousand who had not bowed to Baal or kissed his image (1 Kings 19:18). None of these faithful persons apparently were known by those in the palace or in the nation at large, but they steadfastly refused to worship any of this Baal nonsense. But the Lord knew how they were and he heard their cry for his deliverance.

The New Companion Named Elisha

God told Elijah to "Go back," so he left Sinai and went all the way far to the north where he found Elisha, the son of Shaphat plowing in the fields with his father, on what seemed like a rather large farm, for he was plowing with one of the twelve pair of oxen (1 Kings 19:19). Elijah went up to him and threw the symbol of his office, his mantle, over Elisha. Elisha responded without any fuss or objections, for he left his team of oxen and ran after Elijah (20). However, he did ask Elijah for the privilege of returning briefly to say good-bye to his parents and celebrating the joy of his call into the ministry, Elijah granted his request to briefly return.

But so committed was Elisha to this call of God that he took his yoke of oxen and slaughtered them right there in the field. He also used his plough for firewood to cook the meat of the oxen and gave it to all the people who had now heard that he was going full time into the ministry. There would be no turning back if things did not work out; he was in the service of God for keeps. His "tractors" had been slaughtered and his plowing equipment used as firewood to celebrate the fact that this was a complete dedication of his life.

Some years ago I was using this text in Tokyo, Japan and speaking through an interpreter, one of my former students, Mr. Andrew Furuyama. He was a marvelously accurate translator and as I got to this passage, however, he suddenly started to go on and on, presumably interpreting what I had said. I knew I had not said all of that, even though I did not understand Japanese. Suddenly in the midst of this extensive translation he uttered one word I knew – "sukiyaki." I had been told earlier while ministering in Japan that this favorite Japanese dish was often made in the field by the workers or farmers turning the plough share on its side and building a fire under it to heat the meat and the sauce. Then the cut pieces of meat would be picked up by the diners with chop-sticks and dipped in the sauce and eaten. When the Japanese audience head Andrew's translation, they all responded, "Ah so!" This, then, has become my "sukiyaki" passage in the Bible!

Conclusions and Thought Questions

1. When I am despondent and overcome by a sense of failure, what or on whom do I focus my thoughts? How does my action compare or exceed that of Elijah?

2. How important is the role of friendships when I am depressed and deeply despondent over how things have gone for me? Do you have any Elisha friends/companions in your life?

3. How can I prevent depression and a sense of failure? What part does my view of God have in overcoming my lonely or depressed thoughts?

4. How was Ahab more of a hindrance to the ministry than a help? What changed Elijah's response to this royal couple from the first time he visited them in the palace?

Questions for Discussion and Reflection

1. If Elijah had seen such power as fire from heaven in answer to his prayers, why was he so frightened by Jezebel's threats and why did she give him 24 hours-notice instead of carrying out her threat right away?

2. How important is it to receive proper rest, sleep and nourishment in order to carry out the work of God?

3. How real is the ministry of angels today and what should we teach God's people concerning this topic?

Lesson 4

God's Word From Another Prophet

I Kings 20:1-43

The narrative that has centered on the prophet Elijah in 1 Kings 17-19 seems to discontinue its focus on that prophet temporarily and continues instead to teach us more on King Ahab's failure to obey the word of the Lord and how that word stood opposed to Ahab in 1 Kings 20-22. The 1 Kings 20 account describes three campaigns of Israel against the Arameans/Syrians with their king Ben-Hadad II. Actually, there were three Syrian kings who were called Ben-Hadad: the first was seen in the reign of Asa, king of Judah; the second one appears in our episode in 1 Kings 20; the third will appear in 2 Kings 13 during the reign of Jehoahaz. There was no king like King Ahab who received a stronger literary battering in the Bible than he. It was all due to his adamant opposition to the word of Yahweh, which he resolutely stood opposed to in his thick-skulled obtuseness to all that God said.

We are not told when the events in this chapter occurred, but it is most likely they happened somewhere around 860 B.C., for by 853 B.C. Ahab was once again allied with Damascus and nine other Syrian city-states in opposing the Assyrian conqueror Shalmaneser III in the Battle of Qarqar. And it would be in that Campaign that he would try to regain Ramoth-Gilead for Northern Israel, but in which battle Ahab would be killed by a random arrow around 853 - 852 B.C. So we must assume that after the Battle of Qarqar, Israel and Damascus were at war once again.

The Syrian Siege of Samaria – 1 Kings 20:1-25

The Syrian king Ben-Hadad II laid siege to the capital of Northern Israel, Samaria, as he attempted to force King Ahab of Israel into an easy surrender (20:1). Actually, Ben-Hadad had gathered a rather formidable and intimidating force against Ahab to make his point: he had rallied to his cause 32 kings with their horses and chariots and set up a siege against the capital Samaria (1). Then the Syrian king sent "messengers" into the city to dictate the terms of surrender to Ahab (2). Boastfully the Syrian declared through his messengers that "Your silver and gold are mine, and the best of your wives and children are mine" (3). What was Ahab to do in the face of such an overwhelming show of strength? So he timidly acquiesced: "Just as you say, my lord the king. I and all I have are yours" (4).

Ben-Hadad, sensing that all that had gone too easily decided to up the stakes a little higher, for this time he send his messengers with a new demand: "About this time tomorrow I am going to send my officials to search your palace and the houses of your officials. They will seize everything you value and carry it away" (6). Talk about chutzpah? The hubris and gall of Ben-Hadad seemed to know no limits; he wanted not only Ahab's humiliation, but all that he and his officials owned!

Ahab summoned the elders of Israel as he explained to them: this Syrian bully just wants to start a fight; I agreed to his first demand and now he wants everything (7)! The advice of the elders was: "Don't listen to him or agree to his demands" (8). So Ahab told the messengers he would do what was in the first demand, but this second demand was totally out of the question (9). Ahab felt he had to draw the line in the sand somewhere! But that answer did not sit well with the Syrian autocrat. His next message was as nasty an oath as an Aramean can bring upon his enemy. He vowed in effect that when he was finished with Ahab and Israel, there would not be enough dust left in Samaria for each of his troops to have a handful (10). Lamely Ahab was only able to retort to the

Syrian braggadocio something like: "Let's see you do something before you spout off about what you are going to do" (11). Ben-Hadad got Ahab's response while he and his 32 subordinates were getting drunk in their tents (12). The conqueror ordered" "Prepare to attack." (12b).

Things were as bleak and hopeless as they could be. No way was Ahab going to win a battle against 32 other kings plus this Aramean! However, God had been watching and listening, for clear out of the blue he sent a prophet to King Ahab with a divine word:

> "This is what the LORD says: 'Do you see this vast army? I will give it into your hand today, and then you (sg) will know I am the LORD" (13).

Now there was a huge surprise and an almost unbelievable message. Why would God even bother to waste his word on such an obtuse defiant rebel as Ahab? He was in trouble because he had steadfastly refused to heed what God had said in 1 Kings 17-18, But the love, mercy and grace of God kept chasing King Ahab, so God sent his prophet unsolicited and unknown to Ahab that he was coming. Moreover, despite being totally outnumbered by this monarch and his 32 allies, God promised that he would deliver that same horde of opponents into Ahab's hand! But how? Wasn't this contest over weighted in favor of the attackers?

But why, we ask, would God do such a miracle for such a lowlife? It must have been because God wanted Ahab to stand back and watch Yahweh act on his behalf, for he wanted Ahab to recognize the Lord's person and his sovereignty over all events and all governments, since the word "you" was in the singular form here, whereas in in verse 28 the "you" was plural. God was dealing with Ahab the same way as he dealt with Pharaoh of Egypt, when God [3]spectacularly delivered the Israelites from his

---

3 See Daniel I. Block. *The Book of Ezekiel: Chapters 1-24*, Grand Rapids: Eerdmans, 1997, 39.

grasp (Exod 6:6-9; 7:1, 5, 17): he wanted both Pharaoh and Ahab to come to know that he alone was God overall and the One they both should believe and trust as their Lord and Savior. This formula ("that you may know that I am the LORD") was a favorite with the prophet Ezekiel, for he used the verb "to know" in the same formula 54 times and another 18 times in an expanded form of the same saying (e.g., Ezk 21:40).[4] God was extending the invitation for the king to once more come to terms with the powerful word of God and to believe and trust him along with the nation of Israel.

But Ahab had other questions on his mind. "But who will do this?" (14). Ahab was having a hard time getting all of this straight in his mind. God's prophet was still there for him to ask, so he did ask and found out that God would use "the junior officers under the provincial commanders: (14b) to do this. Apparently these young leaders had not been trained militarily (contrary to NIV translation), so even though there was a lack of experience, God would still work through them to his glory. Ahab still had more questions: "Who will start the battle?" (14d). The answer from the prophet was: "You will." Accordingly, Ahab summoned the 232 junior officers under their provincial commanders with the rest of the army for a total of a mere 7,000 Israeli troops (15a). Thus, this motely-crew set out at noon while Ben-Hadad and his 32 allied kings were getting drunk in their tents (16).

Ben-Hadad received word from his scouts that men were advancing from Samaria (17b), to which Ben-Hadad was so sure of an easy victory that he merely ordered if these men come in peace or for war, take them alive (18). As Davis chuckled, "That order could only come from someone with suds on the brain. A panicky horse-ride will sober him up (20b)"[5]

As the word of God had predicted, Israel was able to enjoy an outstanding victory (19-21), The Arameans suffered extremely heavy losses as Ben-Hadad II escaped on horseback with some

---

4   As pointed out by Dale Ralph Davis, *The Wisdom and the Folly: An Exposition of the Book of First Kings.* Ross-shire, Scotland, Christian Focus, 2002, 290, n 8.
5   Dale Ralph Davis, Op, cit., 289.

of his horsemen (20). Moreover, God send after this was all over with another gracious word for the king of Israel: "Strengthen your position and see what must be done, because next spring the king of Aram will attack you again" (22). The Lord is still showing mercy to Ahab, who still does not deserve it, yet Ahab, of course, never once seeks God's help or asks for this inside information or warning.

The Second Aramean Campaign Versus Israel – 1 Kings 20:23-30

That first encounter with Israel must have really sobered the Syrian bully and 32 more kings. In their post-battle debriefing, they knew exactly why they had lost that first contest:

"Their gods are gods of the hills. That is why they were too strong for us. But if we fight them on the plains, surely we will be stronger than they. Do this: Remove all the kings from their commands and replace them with other officers. You must also raise an army like the one you lost – horse for horse and chariot for chariot – so we can fight Israel on the plains. Then surely we will be stronger than they." (23-24).

Well, this was a lot of optimistic advice for an army that had literally been beaten to ribbons. In an attempt to mix theology with military strategy, they credited Israel with possessing "gods [note the plural] of the hills," but who was to say the gods of these 32 plus nations were gods of the level ground with the Living God? No such claim is directly made, but it is inferred. The Arameans now think it was a mistake to go to war with 32 kings, so they urged that they be replaced with "commanders," thereby centralizing Ben-Hadad's command so he could better oversee the next campaign.

Now for the third time in this narrative (13, 22, 28) a prophet, here called this time "a man of God," "draws near" to give the word of God once more. How persistent God is in his mercy to give his word freely, if only Ahab will listen to it

The next battle took place on the plains of Aphek (modern al-Fiq), a city on the eastern side of the Sea of Galilee and in the northern part of Transjordanian district of Bashan, on a road leading through the Jezreel valley to Beth-Shan to Damascus. The Israelites camped opposite the Arameans, presumably south on the hillside of Aphek. However, they were in comparison to the Syrians, who covered the landscape, like "two small flocks of goats" (27). God sent a "man of God" to assure him of a sure victory and to respond to Aram's insult about Israel's God being effective only in the hills. When God intervened, then Israel and the Syrians would both know that he was Lord (13)

A week later the battle began (29) in which the Syrians suffered 100,000 casualties. Meanwhile, the rest of the troops fled seeking refuge in Aphek. However, the wall of the city mysteriously collapsed, killing 27,000 more Syrians (30). Even King Ben-Hadad had fled to this city, and had hidden in a room inside a room. But since he was certain to be found, his advisers suggested a desperate way he could gamble on saving his life. These advisers pointed to the Israelite's reputation of her kings for being kind and honoring treaties. Thus, they proposed Ben-Hadad take a chance and go to the Israelite king dressed in sackcloth and ropes, symbolizing mourning, penitence, and a symbol of submission with the ropes.

Ben-Hadad went to the king of Israel and pled, "Please, let me live." (32). King Ahab answered, "Is he still alive? He is my brother." Ben-Hadad's advisors took this as a good sign and quickly picked up the word "brother" sensing that mercy was being tendered toward the enemy, so the advisors went as they were told to bring Ben-Hadad to ride in Ahab's chariot. (33), whereupon, Ben-Hadad offered to return the cites Aram had captured from Israel as he also extended trading privileges in the Syrian markets of Damascus (34). Then the two kings made a treaty and Ahab set Ben-Hadad free. This treaty was an economic win for Ahab and Israel, but spiritually it underscored

Ahab's moral and spiritual bankruptcy, which meant the Lord would put an end to Ahab's reign.

This chapter ends with a brief, yet and extremely bizarre happening that set up God's great concluding message to Ahab (35-37), which contest had always been a conflict between the prophet and King Ahab. How persistent God is in his mercy to give his word freely, if only Ahab will listen to it. Now for the third time in this narrative (13, 22, 28) a prophet, here called this time "a man of God," "draws near" to give the word of God once more. How persistent God is in his mercy to give his word freely, if only Ahab will listen to it.

God commanded one of the sons of the prophets to strike his colleague (38-43), but when he refused to strike him, the prophet announced: "For disobeying the LORD, a lion will kill you after you leave." That is what happened to him! The prophet ordered a second man to strike him, and he did so, leaving a wound on the prophet. Thus, the point was this: no matter how outrageous God's commands may seem, death was the penalty for disobedience. Here the was the rule by which Ahab would shortly be judged.

The wounded prophet stationed himself on the roadside he knew Ahab would pass on his way to Samaria (38). He had put a bandage over his eyes to disguise himself. As the king passed by, the wounded prophet called out, beging the king for leniency in his story of an alleged breach of contract (39, Exod 22:7-13). In this assumed case, someone had given the wounded soldier custody of a prisoner of war whom he had somehow let escape his custody. The usual penalty for such dereliction of duty was death or a severe fine of some 75 pounds of silver (2 Sam 14:4-11; 2 Kgs 4:1-7; 6:26-29). This pretending wounded soldier could hardly pay that huge amount of money so death was his only option.

Suddenly the prophet removed his disguise and Ahab recognized him as a prophet (41). Then the king also recognized that the story was fictious and Ahab had set his own doom be releasing his prisoner, viz., Ben-Hadad. The word in vs 42 "should die" is literally "my ban," is a reference to _herem_, i.e., placing under a curse or a ban what now belonged to God alone, just as Achan had done so by taking the items that had been devoted to God at Ai and burying them under his tent (Josh 7). Resentful and furious, Ahab returned to his palace in Samaria (43). Ahab and Israel both were lawbreakers and judgment was coming.

Questions for Thought and Reflection

1. Why do you think that Ahab at first was so concessive to the demands of the Syrian King Ben-Hadad to give up his silver and gold, wives and children? Did he exhibit no trust in God? Why did he finally decide not to accede to Ben-Hadad's command his second time? Did he finally get back his courage and trust in God?
2. How could God have sent an unnamed prophet to wicked King Ahab saying he that he would give that vast army into Ahab's hands? Did Ahab deserve it? Why then did God favor him so greatly in this matter?
3. Why was King Ahab to resort to using the junior officers and not the usual senior ones? What could be the possible explanations for his action?
4. On what grounds did the unnamed man of God (another prophet?) direct Ahab to again challenge the Syrians to conflict?
5. What was so wrong with King Ahab inviting the Syrian King Ben-Hadad to come into his chariot who was wearing sackcloth and ropes? Why the prophetic rebuke? What had the Lord wanted for this hostile king? Why was this the better way to go?

Lesson 5

Buying Into the Moral and Social Ethics of the Day

1 Kings 21:1-29

E lijah the prophet is not mentioned in 1 Kings 20; instead an unnamed prophet appears in 1 Kings 20:12, and later in 20:35, another prophet is identified as "one of the sons of the prophets." So for the moment, Elijah seems to drop out of sight in the story told about the exploits of King Ahab and his infamous wife, Jezebel.

But what is even more disconcerting about this chapter is the fact that 1 Kings 20:1 opens with Ben-Hadad, the king of Aram/ Syria, who is accompanied by 32 other kings, as their horses, chariots and armies besiege Samaria, the capital of northern Israel. Since we have already seen some of the accumulated sins of Ahab and the nation of Israel, we might well have expected that this would be the moment when God would punish this king and queen along with the nation of Israel.

But to our surprise, 1 Kings 20:13 related how God sent a prophet with this remarkable message:

> This is what the LORD says: 'Do you see this vast army? I will give it into your hand today and then you will know that I am the LORD.'

But this was not all that surprises us, for in 1 Kings 20:22, the same (or another) prophet came to King Ahab and said: "Strengthen your position and see what must be done, because by next spring the king of Aram will attack again." Once again the prediction proved to be correct, for as the Israelite army encamped against Syria, Israel's army appeared in comparison to the enemy's forces "like two small flocks of goats, while the Arameans covered the countryside" (27c). The prophet came once more, as he was merely described this time as "the man of God" (28a) and gave another surprising message as well:

> This is what the LORD says: Because the Arameans think that the LORD is a god of the hills and not a god of the valleys, I will deliver this vast army into your hands, and you will know that I am the LORD. (1 Kings 20:28b-d)

Sure enough, the Israelites inflicted a huge loss on the Aramean/ Syrian army as 100,000 enemy troops suffered casualties all in one day. It was not time, at least not as yet, for God to destroy Ahab, for the prophet Elijah had predicted that the divine vengeance would come through King Hazael and not King Ben-Hadad of Aram. But if this judgment was to come by the hands of Ben-Hadad's successor, then why was Ben-Hadad being allowed by God to harass Israel with these attacks? Apparently, it was because God is slow to anger and is long suffering, not willing that any should perish but that all should come to repentance (2 Pet. 3:9, 10). Alas, Ahab did not acknowledge that ADONAI was Lord and Sovereign over all!

To describe what Elijah was doing all this time his name is missing from the record. It would seem that Elijah followed the pattern set by the earlier prophet Samuel, which was one of establishing "schools of the prophets" (1 Sam. 10:5-10; 19, 20) during those periods where we are given no information about Elijah's activities. The sons of the prophets are mentioned in 2 Kings 2, 3, 5, so it is possible that this is what occupied Elijah, and later Elisha, in the days when Ahab was fully occupied defending the country from the Arameans; thus he could not interfere with these two men of God and their schools for the "sons of the prophets." One of these "sons of the prophets" appeared in 1 Kings 20:35, as he read the riot act to Ahab for letting Ben-Hadad go free when God had determined that Ben-Hadad must also die (41-42), but this did not seem to faze Ahab.

Eventually, however, Elijah would be required to face King Ahab personally and pronounce doom over him. This will be the subject of our next exposition of 1 Kings 21.

Text: 1 Kings 21:1-28

Focal Point: V 3, "But Naboth replied, 'The LORD forbid that I should give you [King Ahab] the inheritance of my fathers.'"

Title Of Subject: Buying Into The Moral And Social Ethics Of The Day

Homiletical Keyword: Consequences

Interrogative: What? (were the consequences for Ahab and Jezebel buying into the moral and social ethics of the day?)

Memory Verse: V 3 (Same As The Focal Point Above)

The Outline

I. We Buy Into Coveting When We Sell Ourselves To Wrong Desires21:1-4

II. We Buy Into Evil Alliances When We Choose To Comply With Human Conventions Rather Than The Word Of God21:5-10

III. We Buy Into Becoming A Law To Ourselves When We Defy The Law Of God21:11-16

IV. We Buy Into The Judgment Of God When We Refuse To Change Our Ways21:17-29

The Lesson

We Buy Into Coveting When We Sell Ourselves to Wrong Desires- 21:1-4

Naboth – One Who Feared God

Naboth was an Israelite who owned a piece of family property adjacent to Ahab's summer palace in Jezreel (1). Ahab approached Naboth saying, "Let me have your vineyard to use for a vegetable garden, since it is close to my palace. In exchange I will give you a better vineyard or, if you prefer, I will pay you whatever it is worth" (2).

Naboth responded to this royal request, "The LORD forbid that I should give you the inheritance of my fathers" (3). This was not just worldly-wise good business instincts on Naboth's part, nor was it a response borne out of sentimentality for his father's ancestral land! Naboth was answering in accordance with his religious teaching and the ethics taught in Scripture.

God had taught in the book of Lev. 25:23 that "The land shall not be sold forever, for the land is mine, says the LORD." Also Numbers 36:7 argued, "The sons of Israel shall retain the inheritance of the tribe of their fathers. Ahab did not have what later was to be called in more modern times, "The Right of Eminent Domain." In fact, later on in Ezekiel 46:18, the prince himself could not force anyone out of his property as is possible in certain situations today in the USA.

Other occasions are found in Scripture, where some exercised civil disobedience as Naboth did here. Such was the case of Daniel's three friends, Shadrach, Meshach and Abednego in Daniel 3. They flat out refused to obey the king's command, that when they heard the music playing, they were to fall down in worship of the image he had set up (Dan 3:14-15), They courageously answered the Babylonian King Nebuchadnezzar:

"O Nebuchadnezzar, we do not need to defend ourselves

before you in this matter. If we are thrown into the blazing furnace, the God we serve is able to save us from it, and he will rescue us from your hand, O king. But even if he does not, we want you to know, O king, that we will not serve your gods or worship the image of gold you have set up." (Dan 3:16-18)

Likewise, Peter and John refused to stop preaching the Gospel when the Sanhedrin required it (Acts 4:18), for submission to God topped any requirement to submit to the civil governments of that day, or in any other day! Therefore, in such clear cases, civil disobedience was the correct path to take. We too in our day must judge whether it is right to obey a civil order, that clearly violates what God has taught in his word, or to obey God's orders.

Ahab – One Who Wanted to Get His Own Way

So Naboth was taking his stand on the word of God. He argued: "The LORD forbid" that I should give my inheritance to you, Ahab. That was that, for when God had spoken, all other speeches were moot. Naboth would not be persuaded otherwise, either by money, political clout, intimidation, promise of gain, or the prospect of a better property. His argument was that he was not at personal liberty to accept the king's offer, for he was bound by the word of God.

This did not please King Ahab, for he went home "sullen and angry," because Naboth the Jezreelite had refused to sell his land to him (3). Ahab must have been in the habit of pouting over disappointments, for after he was rebuked by one of the "sons of the prophets" for letting Ben-Hadad go free, the Scriptures recorded that "sullen and angry the king of Israel went to his palace in Samaria (20:4) . Here in Jezreel, he flopped on his bed, where he remained sulking and refusing to eat (4).

We conclude, therefore, that it is no sin or wrong to defy a human government if it requires of us something that manifestly clashes with the word of God. On the other hand, the believer must be a pattern and model of a law-abiding citizen, so long as the claims God makes on us are not infringed. The moral law of God (e.g., in the Ten Commandments or in the Holiness Law in Deut. 18-20) reflects the character of God and therefore these laws were as permanent as God is eternal. The civil law and the ceremonial law were illustrative of the abiding principles found in the moral law of God.

We Buy Into Evil Alliances When We Choose to Comply With Human Conventions Rather Than the Word of God – 21:5-10

Jezebel – Pretender to the Comfort of Ahab

When Ahab's wife Jezebel saw how distressed and angry her husband was (21:5), and why it was that he had refused to eat, she swung into the kind of action that, apparently, she had learned from observing her father Ethbaal, king of Sidon. She would see that the king's demands were carried out, for after all, he was the king! Who or what would stop her?

Ahab carefully deleted all references to the divine law of God as Naboth somewhat explained to his wife Jezebel why Naboth had refused to sell his vineyard. Ahab must have known better, for he could have explained to Jezebel what God had taught in Lev. 25:23? But, no, Ahab made it appear as if it were a case of an outright refusal and merely belligerent intransigence on the part of Naboth in accepting the offer from his king.

Jezebel's Strategy

After Jezebel had roundly castigated her husband for acting more like a mouse than a king (7), she put her plan into action. She said she would get that vineyard, and sure enough, that is what she did (7c).

First of all she used forgery as a tool, for she wrote letters in Ahab's name and placed his seal on the letters (8a), but the letters came from her, not Ahab. Further, in an act of outright and deliberate hypocrisy, she called for a day of fasting (9), thereby conveying the impression to the populace that some horrible wickedness had occurred in the nation that threatened the city with divine judgment if they did not get to the bottom of this blatant sin – as if she cared whether God was pleased or upset. Then she resorted to perjury, for she found "two scoundrels" (10a), and induced them to bear false witness against Ahab. (10b)

Again, A W. Pink hit the nail on the head as he commented:

Here was a woman who sowed sin with both hands. She not only led Ahab deeper into iniquity, but she dragged the elders and nobles of the city into the mire of her Devil-inspired crime. She made the sons of Belial, the false witnesses, worse than they were before. She became both a robber and a murderer filching from Naboth both his good name and heritage. (*The Life of Elijah*, p. 258)

Jezebel is still remembered in the Biblical record as late as the writing of the book of Revelation 2:20. When writing to the congregation of Thyatira, John the apostle said: "Nevertheless, I have this against you: You tolerate that woman Jezebel, who calls herself a prophetess. By her teaching, she misleads my servants into sexual immorality and eating food sacrificed to idols." Thus, this monstrous woman of the apostle John's day exhibited striking parallels with the Jezebel of Ahab's day, which occurred sometime around 90 C.E. Jezebel's name is variously rendered as meaning a "chaste virgin," but also as "dunghill!"

We Buy into Becoming a Law to Ourselves When We Defy The Law of God – 21:11-16

Partial Obedience to the Law of God as a Pretense

Jezebel and her henchmen made a pretense of obeying the law of God by making sure there were two witnesses to Naboth's alleged crime. The Scriptures had taught such in Numbers 35:30 and Deut. 17:6; 19:15. But at the same time, these two dudes had no compunctions about lying, which Scripture also warned about; they just blatantly said they heard Naboth curse both God and the king (13b). Once again, Scripture did warn against both of these sins, first about cursing God and the king in Exodus 22:27 or just about cursing God in Leviticus 13:16. But even if the charge were true, that would not mean that the property reverted to the king, for that happened only in the case of treason. In the case of the two scoundrels, the property of such convicted criminals would be forfeited to the Lord, not to the king (Deut. 13:16). Moreover, even though it was Naboth who was charged with the crime, Naboth's sons, who would have become the proper heirs at Naboth's death, were also killed (2 Kings 9:26). All of this was nothing less than using murder as an excuse for wrongfully taking possession of what did not rightfully belong either the king or the queen. It was all pure politics and perjury!

The Commandments Broken by Jezebel

Jezebel had led the nation, its elders, nobles and people, into committing a violation of six of the Ten Commandments. Not only had she made Baal and Asherah the competing gods in Israel, but now she made Ahab's request higher than God's demands, and thus broke the first commandment of not having any other gods beside the Lord. Then she took the name of the Lord, the third commandment lightly, as the two rogues testified in the name of God that they heard Naboth curse God and the king. This was followed by the murder of Naboth and his sons, a violation of the sixth law of God. They violated the eighth commandment when they stole his good name and reputation and went against the ninth commandment as the men under the direction of Jezebel also gave false testimony. Finally, Ahab coveted his neighbor's land, and thus breached the tenth commandment as well. What a record for wickedness, all from the hands of those who were to see that justice was done in the land and the people were treated fairly.

We Buy into the Judgment of God When We Refuse

to Change Our Ways – 21:17-29

Enter The Prophet Elijah

Now that Naboth and his sons were dead, Jezebel urged her husband Ahab to go down and take possession of the vineyard (16). As Ahab entered the former property of Naboth, the Lord commanded his servant Elijah to go meet Ahab, where he had gone to take possession (17-18). God's word to Ahab was short, crisp and cryptic: "This is what the LORD says: 'Have you not murdered a man and seized his property?' Then say to him: "This is what the LORD says: 'In the place where the dogs licked up Naboth's blood, dogs will lick up your blood – yes, yours.'"

The place where Naboth was executed was outside the city walls (19), but that would be the same place where Ahab's blood would be licked up as well.

Ahab did not seem at first the least bit repentant, for he quipped to Elijah, "So, you have found me, my enemy!" (20a). Elijah retorted, "I have found you, because you have sold yourself to do evil in the eyes of the LORD" (20b). Elijah continued with his doom's day judgment against Ahab by saying that the Lord would bring disaster on Ahab and on his descendants, cutting off every male in his household (21b). Ahab's dynasty would end up just as Jeroboam's and Baasha's had, because of their personal sin and the sin they had caused Israel to fall into. Moreover, Jezebel would be devoured by the dogs near the wall of Jezreel (23). Those of this household that died in the city the dogs would eat and those who died in the countryside, the birds would eat (24). The judgment was stern and it was from God.

Ahab's Repentance

Even though, as Scripture says, "There never was a man like Ahab, who sold himself to do evil in the eyes of the LORD, urged on by Jezebel his wife" (25a), and even though he "behaved in the vilest manner by going after idols, like the Amorites the LORD drove out before Israel," (26), yet when he heard these words, "He tore his clothes, put on sackcloth and fasted. He lay in sackcloth and went round meekly" (27).

The utterly amazing thing that transpired then was God sent his word to Elijah once again (28), saying,

> "Have you noticed how Ahab has humbled himself before me?
> Because he has humbled himself, I will not bring this disaster in
> his day, but I will bring it on his house in the days of his son."

How could God do a thing such as this? Would this not make the prophet's predictions into falsehoods? The answer to this inquiry is one in which we must distinguish between those predictions that have an unstated "unless" (e.g., "if you do not repent and humble yourself") and those that are fulfilled by God himself. Promises like the Abrahamic, Davidic, and New Covenants, are absolute and unconditional as to any dependence on mortals, because they are based on the fact that God himself will fulfill what he has said in them. Consider the case of Jeremiah 18:7-10, where the prophet Jeremiah predicted disaster against the nation of Judah, but if they would relent, then God would not bring his threatened judgment on them. The same was true for individuals. God sincerely wants all men to repent despite the amount and depth of their sins, for he will forgive them. What a gracious God!

Conclusions

1. It grieves our Lord when we steadfastly refuse to humble ourselves and to repent of our sins against him.
2. We must avoid all evil associations that will put us into compromising situations to do evil.
3. God and his word alone form the norm today for what is right, just, and good, for there is no other way to determine how then we should live.
4. When we sell ourselves to do evil, the ropes of sin continue to bind us from one excess to another unless we simply cry out to God in humble repentance and receive his forgiveness.

Questions for Thought and Reflection

1. What standard shall we use in our deciding what is right and what is wrong?
2. What is so phony about persons using part of the Bible to validate their case, but openly violating what other parts of the Bible say?
3. Was Ahab guiltless since his wife really did most of the evil deeds?
4. How can we avoid threatened judgment once it has been given by God?

Lesson 6

Failing to Listen to the Word of The Lord

1 Kings 22:1- 2 Kings 1:18

Elijah and Elisha

A new era of peace began for Israel and Judah, for there were three years in which there was no war between Israel and Aram/Syria or between Israel and Judah (1 Kings 22:1). In that third year, King Jehoshaphat of Judah went down into the northern ten tribes of Israel to visit the king of Israel. By that time, Jehoshaphat had grown strong in the Lord, indeed he also was strong with respect to the kingdoms around him (2 Chron. 17:1-19). Yet, he had also arranged a marriage alliance with King Ahab and Queen Jezebel by uniting in marriage the Israelite royal couple's daughter Athaliah to Jehoshaphat's son Jehoram (2 Chron. 18:1), a sign of weakness and a sure sign of coming trouble. Clearly, this was not pleasing to the Lord.

It was about this time that King Ahab had planned a sumptuous feast for Jehoshaphat in northern Israel, at which he proposed a joint military venture by both Israel and Judah to recapture the city the Arameans had taken from Israel, the city of Ramoth-Gilead. The prophet Jehu rebuked Jehoshaphat for joining in this military venture (2 Chron. 19:1). Moreover, the prophet Eliezer also rebuked him for his later joining Jehu's son and successor to the throne of Israel, King Ahaziah, in an unapproved shipbuilding venture at Ezion-Geber (2 Chron. 20:36).

Jehoshaphat was a good king, but he was very easily led off the path of righteousness as he endeavored to please everyone. Even though he often repented later for his hasty indiscretion, he had to be taught and forgiven over and over again. All too often he acted, then he checked with the Lord to see if what he had done was correct!

Text: 1 Kings 22:1- 2 Kings 1:18

Focal Point: 2 KINGS 1:6c, 16b, "Is it because there is no God in Israel that you are sending men to consult Baal-Zebub?"

Title of Subject of the Lesson: "Failing To Respond To The Word Of God"

Homiletical Keyword: Evidences

Interrogative: What? (Are The Evidences Wherein They In Their Day And We In Ours Fail To Respond To The Word Of God?)

Memory Verse: Same As Focal Point – 2 Kings 1:6, 16

The Outline

   I. In Our Belittling Of The Word Of God – 22:1-12

   V. In Our Pervasive Opposition To The Word Of God -22:13-28

   VI. In Our Hardened Conscience To The Word Of God – 22:29-40

   VII. In Our Refusal To Seek God In Times Of Calamity –2 Kings 1:1-18

The Lesson

In Our Belittling Of The Word Of God –
I Kings 22:1-12

Ahab Invites Jehoshaphat to Join Him 22:1-4

King Ahab had repented and humbled himself (I Kings 21:27-29), but now that he was on his feet again, this repentance all seemed to have been forgotten. Instead, he turned to an alliance that he proposed with Jehoshaphat as the arm he could lean on, in place of depending on the Lord. Actually, 2 Chronicles 18:2, the word "urged him" could also be rendered by the words that Ahab "seduced him" (also rendered in Deut. 13:6 as "enticed"), saying, "Will you go with me to fight against Ramoth Gilead?" (1 Kings 22:4). You would think that by now Jehoshaphat would be wise to Ahab's requests to join him in his ungodly ventures, but once again Jehoshaphat naively first agreed to join with him before he consulted the Lord.

The Call of an Adonai Prophet, Son of Imlah –
Micaiah -22:5-12

Jehoshaphat's response was unequivocal: "I am as you are, my people as your people, my horses as your horses." But he then suddenly had second thoughts, for he now belatedly recalled that he must "First, seek the counsel of the LORD?" (5). Meanwhile, King Ahab had learned nothing from the total ineffectiveness of the prophets of Baal and Asherah, for he brought together his own prophets that Jezebel had schooled, the prophets of Baal, about 400 of them (6), and consulted with them on whether he should go up to attack Ramoth-Gilead. Naturally, the answer of these 400 "yes"-men was "Go!" (6c). But Jehoshaphat asked, "Is there not a prophet of the LORD [ADONAI] here whom we can inquire of?" (7). Jehoshaphat knew there was a real difference between those who faked giving the word of ADONAI and those who knew the Lord and respected his word and told the truth.

Ahab's argument with Jehoshaphat was that Ramoth-Gilead belonged to Israel, yet Israel had done nothing to retake it away from Aram/Syria all these years. The people of Israel could no longer be silent; furthermore, that city could serve as a possible base for future menaces and invasions of Israel, so what was holding Israel back from attacking them – or so Ahab must have thought?

Even though Jehoshaphat had promised to go with Ahab to attack Ramoth-Gilead, he wanted a confirming word from a genuine ADONAI prophet. Ahab knew of only one such prophet in his realm, Micaiah, son of Imlah; but he hated him because he never gave Ahab favorable prophecies, so he had him imprisoned in Samaria (8). Nevertheless, Ahab sent for Micaiah. While they waited for Micaiah to come, 400 prophets of Baal were urging the two kings to "Go, for the LORD will give [Ramoth-Gilead] into the king's hand" (6c). Thus, it was to humor Jehoshaphat that Ahab had sent for Micaiah, but he expected very little good to come from the exercise. Anyway, the score stood at 400 to 0!

As they waited for Micaiah's arrival, the two kings, dressed in their royal robes, sat on their thrones in the entrance to the gate of Samaria, with all the 400 prophets of Baal prophesying before them (10). To fill in the time, one of those 400 prophets, Zedekiah son of Kenaanah, had made iron horns, which he used in a sort of religious drama, as he no doubt danced about saying, "This is what ADONAI says: 'With these you will gore the Arameans until they are destroyed'" (11). With this, all the prophets agreed, saying the same thing (12). It was one pathetic display of "yes-men" filling in the time.

In Our Pervasive Opposition to the Word of God –

22:13 – 28

The Present Request Was Insincere – 22:13-16

Messengers were sent to summon Micaiah from prison, but they tried to clue Micaiah in to the fact that, so far, all the other prophets had agreed 100 % with the advice to go and attack Ramoth-Gilead, so he would be wise to speak favorably of the project in that same way (13). Micaiah, however, protested that he could only say what God had told him to say (14).

When Micaiah arrived, at first he spoke facetiously and perhaps in a tone of voice that gave away his true feelings by saying, "Attack and be victorious" (15b), but he did not preface his words with the key prophetic formula of ADONAI prophets by saying, "Thus says the LORD/ADONAI."

Ahab tried to represent himself as one who was open and ready to act on any declaration from ADONAI, as he remonstrated with Micaiah by perfunctorily saying these words: "How many times must I make you swear to tell me nothing but the truth [and to do it] in the name of the LORD?" (16). This verse is dripping with sarcasm and irony, if not hypocrisy as well! Ahab is one big "phony."

A Parable of the Scattered Flock on the Hills – 22:17-18

Micaiah then got serious as he described how he saw all Israel scattered all over the hills like sheep without a shepherd (17). The LORD then said, "These people have no master. Let each one go home in peace" (17b).

Ahab did not miss Micaiah's point: he was that "shepherd" and Israelites were the "sheep." His rejoinder was directed, not to Micaiah, but to Jehoshaphat: "Didn't I tell you that he never prophesies anything good about me, but only bad?" (18). Ahab would lose his life in this battle, but he still mocked the word of God from God's servant Micaiah. Perhaps Micaiah had on his mind the text from Numbers 27:17 - "[A man] shall go out before [Israel] and come in before them, and he shall lead them out and bring them in; that the congregation of the LORD may not be as sheep which have no shepherd."

Ahab's Chosen Falsehood Will be The Means of His Own Ruin – 22:19-28

Micaiah gave the divine word to King Ahab in vv. 19-20. (There is nothing like this in the rest of the Tanakh.) He said:

> I saw the LORD sitting on his throne with all the host of heaven standing around him on right and on his left. And the LORD said, 'Who will entice Ahab into attacking Ramoth Gilead and going to his death there?' One suggested this, and another that. Finally, a spirit came forward, stood before the LORD, and said, 'I will entice him.' "By what means?" the LORD asked. 'I will go out and be a lying spirit in the mouths of all his prophets,' he said. 'You will succeed in enticing him,' said the LORD. 'Go and do it.'

The Lord had mingled among the 400 prophets a spirit of confusion. Thus, King Ahab, who had heaped up sin upon sin, was now set by the determinate will of God as agreed to by God's divine council that, indeed, destruction should come upon Ahab. The only question was the means or the method by which this destruction should come. It would be by a "lying spirit" that would be put in the mouths of all Ahab's false prophets. This judicial act of God would be one in which he permitted the false calculations of human hearts to be the instrument for ruining Ahab, for he who had lost any concept of distinguishing between the true word of God and all the imitations of that same powerful word of God by his false prophets, would himself be tricked by a similar substitution for the real word of God.

Once in a while, God permits evil to be the means by which evil is punished, for this same idea can be found in Isaiah 19:14 —"The LORD has poured into [the wise men of Egypt] a spirit of dizziness; they make Egypt stagger in all she does," or in 2 Thessalonians 2:11-12—"For this reason, God send them a powerful delusion, so that they will believe a lie, and so that all will be condemned who have not believed the truth, but have delighted in wickedness," Therefore, Ahab and his people who did not trust the word of God were exactly like those of Romans 1:24-28, where "God gave them up to the lusts of their own hearts." If they loved deceit they would themselves be deceived!

Judgment also fell on Zedekiah, son of Kenaanah, the chief prophet of the 400 false prophets, as Micaiah had predicted. For when Micaiah said that God has sent a lying spirit in the mouths of these 400 pretenders of true prophecy, Zedekiah went up to Micaiah and slapped him in the face (23-24). Zedekiah asked impudently, "Which way did the spirit from the LORD go when he went from me to speak to you?" (24b). Micaiah replied, "You will find out on the day you go to hide in an inner room" (25).

King Ahab had had enough of Micaiah and his messages, so he sent him back to jail in the care of Amon, the ruler of the city of Samaria, and to Joash the son of the king. They were to put Micaiah in prison and fed him nothing but bread and water until Ahab came home in his expected victory at Ramoth-Gilead (27).

Micaiah's retort was this: "If you ever return safely, the LORD has not spoken through me." He added: "Mark my words, all you people!" Surely, that must have shaken some of the more sensitive souls who were there that day, and even more when the events unfolded just as Micaiah had predicted they would.

In Our Hardened Consciences to the Word of God – 22:29-40

Ahab Killed at Ramoth-Gilead – 22:29-40

The word of God must have had some impact on King Ahab, for he volunteered to go into battle in a disguise, instead of the insignias of his royalty, (29) and to let Jehoshaphat be the sole individual who was dressed as a king in this battle against Aram. But it is impossible to hide from God! For unbeknown to either Ahab or Jehoshaphat, the king of Aram had ordered his 32 chariot commanders the following instruction: "Do not fight with anyone, small or great, except the king of Israel" (31b). Naturally, when these charioteer-drivers saw King Jehoshaphat, they concluded that he was the King of Israel, so they turned to attack him. That must have been a sober moment for the king of Judah, as he cried out that he was not the king of Israel (32). Somehow, in the providence of God, the Syrian charioteer officers concluded that this was not the king of Israel and quit pursuing him (33). Jehoshaphat had a narrow escape from death, despite his sinful compromising with the men of evil (vv. 32-33). When this king of Judah returned home to Jerusalem, he was met by another ADONAI prophet, this one named Jehu, the son of Hanani, who asked him:

> "Should you help the wicked and love those who hate the LORD? There is, however, some good in you, for you have rid the land of the Asherah poles and have set your heart on seeking God." (2 Chron. 19:2-3)

But God's plan was not frustrated just because Ahab rigged up a disguise, for an Aramean soldier "drew his bow at random and hit the king of Israel between the opening made by sections in his armor (34), piercing his heart! Seeing he was wounded, he instructed his chariot driver to "wheel around and get [me] out of the fighting, [for I] have been wounded" (34c). The battle raged on all day long with the king propped up in his chariot facing the Arameans, while his blood trickled down on the floor of the chariot (35; cf. 1 Kings 21:19). I wonder what went through the mind of King Ahab in those ebbing moments of life?

The Prophecy Fulfilled to the Letter – 22:37

Just as the sun was setting, a cry went up for everyone to return to his own town in Israel (36). Tragically, King Ahab by now had died, and as predicted, after they got home, they washed his chariot at a pool outside of Samaria and there the dogs licked up his blood (38). God's word was true and the word of the 400 charlatans, from those false prophets of Ahab, was shown to be bankrupt and obviously false.

Jehoshaphat Learns Another Lesson – 22:41-50

This Judean king, Jehoshaphat, ruled Judah for thirty-five years, starting when he was twenty-five years old (41). He modeled his life after the good aspects of his "father" King Asa, for he did not stray from what God had taught in his word (43). He did, however, fail to remove the high places (43c) even though he cleared the land of the male prostitutes' shrines that his father had left standing in the land (46).

But Jehoshaphat's open naiveté was evident in yet another situation in vv. 48-49. He had commissioned the construction of a fleet of trading ships to go to Ophir to obtain gold apparently designed to imitate the merchant-fleet that Solomon had built years ago for the same purpose (1 Kings 9:2, 6). But Jehoshaphat's merchant marines never set sail. Instead, these ships were wrecked in a storm in the harbor at Ezion-Geber (48), because Jehoshaphat had compromised the whole project with an alliance with yet another Israelite king. He had entered into this ship-building enterprise in alliance with the new king of Israel, Ahab's son, named Ahaziah (2 Chron. 20:35-36). But God sent another ADONAI prophet, named "Eliezer son of Dodavahu," into his life. Eliezer prophesied that "Because you have made an alliance with Ahaziah, the LORD will destroy what you have made" (2 Chron. 20:37). Thus, the ships were wrecked and were not able to set sail to trade (2 Chron. 20:37c). The storm that wrecked the ships was a divine punishment from God for an apostate action by this king. Jehoshaphat had learned his lesson, for he turned down a later second request for a joint ship-building effort with the Israelite king (49).

In Our Refusal to Seek God in Our Times of Calamity -2 Kings1:1-18

In the Disregard for Learning From the Past – 2 Kings 1:1-2

The new king of northern Israel, the son of Ahab, Ahaziah, had accidentally fallen through the lattice from the upper story of his palace in Samaria (2 Kings 1:2), so he sent messengers to consult Baal-Zebub, the god of Ekron, to see if he would recover from his fall! This in itself is astounding! One would think that after three and a half years of famine, in which their god Baal, who was supposedly over all dew, rain, and fertility in the land of Israel, had so miserably failed, that such an expose on that god's impotence and failure to even show up, would have doomed his alleged divine status once and for all with the king and his people. Didn't anyone wake up and smell the coffee? How quickly the slaughtered 850 false prophets of Baal and Asherah had been replaced with a whole school of new phonies in Jezebel's seminary. Didn't anyone pay attention to history? What would it take to wake up this nation and people? Were all the lessons given to Ahab and Jezebel lost on the new generation?

1 Kings 22:51-53 summarized the short two-year reign of Ahaziah in Israel by saying, "He did evil in the eyes of the LORD, because he walked in the ways of his father [Ahab] and [his] mother [Jezebel]." Moreover, "He served and worshiped Baal, and provoked the LORD, the God of Israel, to anger, just as his father had done" (53). Ahab and Jezebel had left a real mark on their son!

God Seeks Us Through Calamity – 1:3-8

God was so provoked that he allowed Moab to rebel against Israel (1). This introduced the collapse of the balance of power among the nations with the disappearance of the peace and security Israel had enjoyed for a period of time. So, it is today as well, when God is provoked with nations, churches, families, politicians and theologians, we will see a corresponding dissolution of their spheres of influence and a general lack of success in their ventures. But God was not finished Ahaziah, for he sent him another sign. He allowed him to fall through the lattice from an upper story of the palace in Samaria. Surely this fall would give him time to reflect on the things he had seen and learned about the God of gods during his youthful days in the government of his father and mother! But it was all just useless; Ahaziah showed no sign of humbling of himself before God. On the contrary, he sent messengers to Baal-Zebub, even as God gave Ahaziah additional space and time to repent, for he did not die instantly from his fall. As we said, he had had time on his bed to consider his ways, but his appeal to Baal-Zebub was proof that his soul was in worse shape than his fractured body.

In Ugaritic, a Canaanite language that shares about 60% of its vocabulary with Hebrew, "Zebul" meant "lord, prince," but the Hebrews deliberately misspelled and mispronounced "Zebul" and rendered it instead "Zebub," which meant "flies;" so this god of Ekron was "Lord of the flies" – an auspicious title indeed – one that easily could be "buzzed off!" In this way the writer defamed and stigmatized Baal for what he deserved. Ahaziah should have "swatted" the very idea of consulting Baal-Zebub as a god!

Thus it was that "the angel of the LORD" said to Elijah, "Go up and meet the messengers of the king of Samaria and ask them, 'Is it because there is no God in Israel that you are going off to consult Baal-Zebub, the Philistine god of Ekron [the northernmost of the five cities of the Philistine pentapolis]?" The angel of the Lord in this context is probably a corporeal appearance of Yeshua in bodily form, prior to his incarnation as a baby in Bethlehem. Periodically, Messiah appeared in the Tanakh as the "Angel of the Lord." For example, in Exodus 23:20-21, the Lord said his "name" was "in him," i.e., the Angel of the Lord.

The messengers returned so quickly back to Ahaziah that he questioned why they had returned so soon (5). They replied it was because of the man they had met on the way and what he had said to them. When asked to describe this man, they identified him as having a garment of hair and a leather belt around his waist. King Ahaziah knew instantly that this was none other than Elijah the Tishbite, the nemesis of his family (8b). The message from the Lord that the messengers gave to the king was that he would not get up from his bed; he would certainly die (4).

An Attempt to Put Elijah to Death – 1:9-18

Ahaziah was so enraged that he resolved to put Elijah to death. So, he sent one of his captains with fifty men to apprehend Elijah (9), who was sitting on top of a hill – perhaps the very Mount Carmel where God had sent fire in answer to his prayer (9b). In what must have been a haughty and dictatorial tone, the Israelite captain ordered Elijah, "the Man of God," "Get down." (9c). But Elijah responded, "If I am a man of God, may fire come down from heaven and consume you and your fifty men" (10a). That is what happened immediately! Surely, he must have known that to insult ADONAI's messenger, who spoke with the message from God, was to insult God himself! This would have worked very well of Jezebel too had he thought of it!

But Ahaziah was not moved by his loss, nor did he repent; instead he ordered a second captain and his squad of fifty to demand that this man of God "Come down at once" (11). But the results were the same as they were with the previous captain, so another fifty-one men were consumed by fire (12). Things were really beginning to heat up!

Once more the king sent a third captain and squad of fifty men (for Ahaziah must have been determined to fight on despite his obvious losses), but this captain pled with Elijah to "Please have respect for [my] life and those of [my] men" (13). Then it was that the angel of the LORD gave permission for Elijah to go down with him (15), so Elijah went to see the king.

Elijah repeated the same message he had given to the messengers he had intercepted on the road to Ekron (16). Thus, in accordance with this word from the Lord, Ahaziah died (17). God had acted in the lives of Ahaziah and the first two squads of fifty men each, but God had done this not to placate his prophet, or to gratify Elijah's sense of pride, but to show his power and justice. Hence, all generations of society are warned not to mock God's ministers or his message, because of the words they bring are from God himself: in fact, such mocking of the message and his messengers is itself a form of taking God on personally. But for the fearful and repentant, as in the case of the third captain, who had realized that the judgment had come from God and not Elijah, God was merciful. He used the expression, "fire from heaven," but in this case the word "heaven" was a word that stood for God himself, for it merely avoided the possibility of using God's name in vain. So, God does wait to show mercy to any who will humble themselves under the mighty hand of God, as was true of the third captain.

Conclusions

1. Is it because Israel and we think there is no God in the land, that we carry-on as if God does not hear, see, or act as he has promised?
2. There is a present revelation of the wrath of God as well as a revelation of his wrath in a final day, when it all comes together climactically.
3. Let us beware of making compromising alliances with those who do not love the Lord, for they can often drag us down into the mire of sin.
4. Even though King Jehoshaphat evidenced a lot of pure desire to love and follow the Lord, he was also in need of wisdom from God, to keep him from joining anyone or anything before he would ask for wisdom from God.

Questions for Thought and Reflection

1. How careful should we be in joining in projects and partnerships with unbelievers?
2. Can a random act of shooting an arrow be directed in its aim in the providence of God or was it purely accidental?
3. What was Jehoshaphat's key moral defect? What is a cure for such a problem?
4. How did King Ahab's falsehood turn out to be his undoing?

Lesson 7

Elijah and the Second Coming of Messiah

Malachi 4:5; Luke 9:28-36; Revelation 11:3-19

E lijah not only served his own day and times in a powerful way, but he, under the appointment of God, was designated by the same Lord to be a harbinger and an earnest that would function as a sort of a down-payment on what was yet to be realized in the history of this world in connection with the coming great and dreadful day of the Lord. Elijah, it turns out, more than any other person in the history of the ongoing story of God's plan for the world, demonstrated what could be expected from himself in the end days as well as what could be expected from those leaders who were filled with the Holy Spirit and the power of God!

Accordingly, God would still use Elijah in that future day of the Lord as he had in the past. After all, had not the last prophet of the Tanakh, the prophet Malachi, predicted: "Behold, I will send you Elijah the prophet before the great and dreadful day of the Lord comes?" (Mal. 4:5).

Elijah as a Prototype of the Coming of John
The Immerser

Elijah's work apparently was not finished when our Lord took him up to heaven in a whirlwind. We catch a glimpse of this when

the disciples of Yeshua asked our Lord very directly if the prophet
Elijah was going to come back to earth and precede his second
arrival as the Messiah of Israel: "Why do the scribes say that first
Elijah must come?" Our Lord's answer at first sounded as if it were
a bit of "double-talk," for he replied: "Elijah is coming [present
tense] and he is to restore all things; but I tell you that Elijah has
already come and they did to him whatever they pleased . . . .
Then the disciples understood that he was speaking about John
the Immerser" (Matt. 17:11-13; Mark 9:13). The disciples had
therefore gained an understanding of what the prophecy meant
that Elijah must precede the coming of our Lord, but it seems they
only got a piece of it correct.

But we still need more data before we can understand more
fully what our Lord was pointing to when he mentioned a coming
of Elijah and how John the Immerser fitted into this picture. So,
when John the Immerser was asked straight out if he were Elijah,
his answer was just as straightforward: "No." John was quizzed
further, "Are you a prophet?" Again, he simply answered, "No."
Now they were really puzzled all the more, for they asked in
frustration, "Who are you then?" John's answer was this: "I am
a voice crying in the wilderness; 'Prepare the way of the Lord.'"
(John 1:21). John, of course, was appealing to the prophetic words
of Isaiah 40:3 ("The voice of one calling: in the desert prepare the
way for the LORD ......"). The Immerser was a herald of Messiah,
one who prepared the way for his coming!

It is not to be concluded that there is a contradiction in Yeshua's,
or Scripture's words, or that the text of Scripture, or in the Holy
Spirit who gave the Scriptures, as if they could not make up their
mind on whether John the Immerser was indeed the coming Elijah
or not. For Yeshua added on another occasion: "For all the law
and the prophets prophesied until John [the Immerser]; and if you
are willing to accept it, he is Elijah who is to come" (Matt. 11:13,
14). That clears up part of this puzzle, for Yeshua regarded John
the Immerser as the fulfillment of that prophecy, both in the sense

of one who already fulfilled the prediction about Elijah who was to come, and yet in a more extended sense, John's coming had not completely fulfilled the entire prophecy, for it fell short of the total fulfillment of this divine word in Scripture. This is why it is all the more important that we see in what sense John fulfilled the prophecy, for in order to do that we must also include the pledge the angel made at the announcement of the birth of John the Immerser. John, the angel affirmed, would go forth before the Lord "in the spirit and the power of Elijah" (Luke 1:17). There is the key which helps us to see how John the Immerser could have fulfilled the prediction about Elijah's coming and yet we can also see how John could not have fulfilled everything the prophet Malachi had in mind when he gave his prediction about Elijah future coming.

In order to understand this, we must realize that prophecy in the Bible often has both a "now" aspect and a "not yet" side to its predictions (1 John 3:2). Willis J. Beecher taught much the same when he announced what he called "Generic Predictions," which he carefully defined in this manner:

> "A generic prediction is one which regards an event as occurring in a series of parts, separated by intervals, and expresses itself in language that may apply indifferently to the nearest part, or to the remoter parts, or to the whole – in other words, a prediction which, in applying to the whole of a complex event, also applies to some of its parts."[6]

The idea here is that some prophecies point to a final, climactic event, but often that event is itself part of a previous series of events, all of which participate in or lead up to the climactic event. What embraces this series of parts is not some sort of double sense, i.e., an alleged double meaning of the text of Scripture, or some spiritual or deeper meaning, which escaped the purview of the writer of Scripture, but the fact that at times Scripture's

---

6   Willis J. Beecher, _The Prophets and the Promise_, New York: Crowell, 1905; Grand Rapids, Baker, 1963, p. 130.

teachings comes through persons, things or concepts that had what
is known as a corporate or collective solidarity. Accordingly, to
give an example, the prophecy about the coming "seed" that was
part of God's promise-plan for this world includes in the one word
"seed," not only the promise of a coming One who is the Messiah
(Gal. 3:16), but it often included all who will accept Messiah by
faith and constitute the one people of the promise! Thus, Scripture
would often seem to oscillate between the "one" and the "many"
in its use of terms such as the "seed."

Joel's promise of the "Day of the Lord" is another good
example of such a generic prediction. Peter stood up in front of
the crowd and spoke about the "day of the Lord" on the day of
Pentecost and affirmed: "This is [that which, or] what was spoken
by the prophet Joel" (Acts 2:16-21; Joel 2:16). That seemed to
have settled the matter as far as Joel's audience was concerned
– Pentecost was the day Joel had meant when he spoke of the
"day of the Lord." However, note that as much as eight centuries
after Joel made his prediction, Peter spoke these same words on
the day of Pentecost (*Shavuot*); however he applied only the first
two verses of that prediction, but he did not include "wonders in
the heavens and on earth, blood and fire and billows of smoke."
Nor was the "sun turned into darkness" or "the moon to blood."
Even though those words were part of the prophecy, they were not
fulfilled on the day of Pentecost – there was more to come which
Pentecost did not complete!

This same point can be made about other prophecies, such as
the ones about the coming of the awful Antichrist. Already John
had warned that "many antichrists have come" (1 John 2:18), even
though Antiochus Epiphanes IV had appeared and met part of the
fulfillment. Thus, just as a Messianic line of David's descendants
came one after the other until Messiah came, so there would be a
line of power-grabbers and God-haters throughout history, each
who could be truthfully called the "Antichrist" until the final one
in that line arrived in a future day.[7] In this way Elijah would indeed
come before the great and dreadful day of the Lord yet in the future!

---

7   Walter c. Kaiser, Jr, "The Prophetic use of the Old Testament in the New," in *The Uses of the Old Testament in the New*, Chicago: Moody, 1985, pp 61-100.

Elijah the Prophet Appeared During Ministry of Yeshua

It happened just one week after the famous incident that took place at Caesarea-Philippi, where the disciple Peter had made his great confession of our Lord in answer to Yeshua's question to his disciples, "Who do you say I am?" Peter famously blurted out, "You are Messiah, the Son of the living God" (Matt. 16:16). Yeshua praised Peter for his correct answer, but then cautioned him to remember that he was able to say this, not as a result of his own ingenuity, but as the result of a revelation from his Father in heaven.

One week later, Yeshua took Peter, James and John up into a high mountain by themselves as our Lord began to fortify himself for the great spiritual and physical ordeal that was to take place in Jerusalem, where he would be hauled off to be crucified. Once on that mountain, Yeshua began to prepare for this crisis by entering into prayer. As he was praying, suddenly he was transfigured right before their eyes (Matt. 17:1-8; Mark 9:2-8; Luke 9:28-36). So radiant was the change that took place in Yeshua as he was praying, and as he was transfigured in front of the three disciples, that "his face shone as the sun" (Matt. 17:2). In that moment, the *Shekinah* glory broke out on the One who himself was and is the Glory of God. Thus, this outburst of brilliance was but a brief anticipation of that glory that was soon to be his on a permanent basis – the glory he had with the Father, but which glory he had laid aside voluntarily, that is until he had finished the work God the Father had sent him to accomplish on earth.

Yeshua's clothes became dazzling white and bright as a flash of lightning. Such a brilliance must have been resplendent against the backdrop of the dark blue sky. In so doing, our Lord provided another reminder of those numerous appearances of the Son of Man throughout the Tanakh, such as the pillar of fire by night, the cloud of glory by day, the burning bush, that did not consume the bush, the thunder and lightning on Sinai, along with those times when the Lord fought for Israel.

All of a sudden, two men appeared with Yeshua: Moses and the prophet Elijah! If we should ask, "Why these two men?" The answer undoubtedly was to affirm the glory, dignity, and assured success of our Lord before he faced the darkest hour he or this world had seen up to that point. The enormous shame, ignominy, and disgrace needed to be counterbalanced and set over against the blazing glory that was anticipated in the triumphal conclusion of Yeshua in his death and resurrection in Jerusalem.

Moses appeared with our Lord as one who represented the one who was the bringer of the Torah (Law); he who had the power to accomplish such through the Father, as well as to turn the waters into blood and to smite the earth with every plague. Elijah, on the other hand, was the one who under God the Father was the one who was given the power to shut up the heavens so that it did not rain. In many ways he was at the head of the whole line of prophets These two key mortals from Israel's past entered into conversation with Yeshua, the Messiah, on that mountain in the presence of the three disciples.

But what could their conversation have been about? Luke tells us that the topic of their conversation was this – it was nothing less than the "exodus" or "departure" that Yeshua was shortly to accomplish in Jerusalem (Luke 9:31). Great leaders talk with a great God on great topics! Such a topic of conversation, then, is no surprise, for the salvation of the two representatives as well as the three disciples was dependent, just as much as our own salvation, on what was to take place shortly in Jerusalem. Their only hope lay exactly where ours lays – in the work of Messiah on their behalf. Had Yeshua not died for all our sin, all the saving grace that had been promised in the pre-cross moments in a proleptic way would have been ineffective and valueless!

Moses and Elijah were not singled out because they were some sort of super saints or that they were mortals who were sinless. In fact, it was already recorded in Scripture how petulant Moses had been on occasion, and how fretful and cowardly Elijah had acted subsequent to the Mount Carmel event. But great men, as we noted already, talk about great themes and so they together entered into the theme of redemption which Messiah would soon accomplish in a matter of days.

Moses may well have dwelt on how Yeshua must die as the lamb of God, the goat whose blood was shed on the Day of Atonement. True, the blood of bulls and goats could never take away sin (Heb. 10:1-2), but neither did the first covenant claim that was possible or teach that the blood mentioned in Leviticus did take away sins. Instead, it argued that forgiveness was available as the gift of God; the sin offerings that accompanied divine forgiveness were merely pictures of that special work which was yet to come in the shed blood of Yeshua on the cross, the Roman execution stake.

No less exciting must have been the contribution from the prophet Elijah. He too most assuredly must have contributed to this elevated conversation by talking about the glory that should now belong to God the Father, the glory that would come when Yeshua had accomplished all that God the Father had planned from eternity. The same glory that had thundered down on Mount Carmel. The glory which Elijah had caught a glimpse of at the mouth of the cave on Mount Sinai as he was summoned in his despondent mood to watch the majesty of the glory of the God of all might and power! This was the same glory that would now break out with the Resurrection and radiate all over the earth with unsurpassed brilliance and majesty.

All that Moses and Elijah had talked about with the Lord, and much more, was all well known to our Lord, for, after all, it was he who had first given it to them under the inspiration of the Holy Spirit. Nevertheless, these were the identical topics that must have strengthened and gladdened the heart of our Lord as he now faced the darkest moment that heaven ever has or ever will face.

What Moses and Elijah experienced on the Mount of Transfiguration was a review of what they had known in their walk with God as well as an earnest or harbinger of what was to come in the future. Of all the possible topics that that conversation on the mount could have been about, all would have been dwarfed by the magnitude of Yeshua's death and his resurrection centered in this conversation about his "departure" or "exodus."

In the New Testament, there are some 175 passages that focus on the death of Yeshua. The point must be made, therefore, that the closer we get to his sacrificial death on a cross in our theology and its emphases, the closer we come to the heart and center of our faith in Messiah, and his triumphal conclusion to all he has planned for those who love him.

The Appearance of the Two Witnesses in Revelation 11:3-19

There is one more episode in our study of the life of Elijah we must examine in order to complete our study of Elijah; it is Revelation 11:3-19. Of course, some believers tend to get nervous when the subject of study becomes the book of Revelation, but such nervousness is unnecessary, for the final book in the New Testament is primarily a book of worship; it is "the revelation of Yeshua the Messiah" (Rev. 1:1). The scene that dominates the whole book of Revelation is the throne of God (Rev. 4-5).

But what is of special interest to us is the eleventh chapter of Revelation, which records the narrative about the two witnesses. It is true, of course, that this episode does not say that one of the witnesses is Elijah the Tishbite, but it does say that "these men have power to shut the sky so that it will not rain during the time they are prophesying and they have power to turn waters into blood and to strike the earth with every kind of plague as often as they want" (Rev. 11:6). This description strongly suggests that Moses and Elijah are empowered by God to come back to earth again as seen in the powers they will be able to use.

The message of Revelation 11 is that two men will stand up in Jerusalem and preach repentance for 1,260 days (approximately three and a half years). These two witnesses are the same two who are pictured in the book of Zechariah (4) standing before the Lord to serve God. So the two witnesses will stand before God to witness for him just before the great climax in history arrives. The interesting point is that the emphasis of Zechariah 4:3 is precisely where it was in the lives of Elijah and the John the Immerser. Zechariah announced in that text: "Not by might, nor by power, but by my Spirit, says the LORD of Hosts." And that is where the matter still rests in our day as well. It is still a matter of the infilling of the Holy Spirit and the power from God that we today are able to carry out the mission of the Messiah (cf. Luke 1:17). Did not Elijah's successor, the prophet Elisha, pray for a double portion of Elijah's spirit (2 Kings 2:9)?

The story does not end there, however. These two witnesses in that final day were not unopposed, for suddenly the "beast" in Revelation 11:7 appears. He is easily identified as "the man of lawlessness" (2 Thess. 2:3) or as the "little horn" in Daniel 7:21. This monster will come up from the Abyss to attack, oppose, overpower, and kill the two witnesses who will be preaching the gospel. Not only will he kill them, but he will leave their bodies in the streets of Jerusalem to rot (Rev. 11:8). So relieved will the men and women of every people, tribe, language and nation be, as they stare and gawk at their dead bodies, that they will send gifts to one another (Rev. 11:9, 10).

After the bodies had lain in the streets for three and a half days while all this celebrating and rejoicing over the deaths of these two ministers of the gospel is going on, suddenly, in the midst of all the partying and giving of gifts to each at the success of silencing these two witnesses, God will grant his two witnesses life once again. We can only imagine the shock and consternation that this sudden change in their vitality will bring world-wide.

This will be followed by a loud voice that will direct them to "Come up here!" (Rev. 11:12) as they disappear from mortal's sight and ascend up to heaven in a cloud, as their enemies look on such a spectacular event presumably with gasps and mouths opened wide in amazement!

Now in that very same hour there will be an earthquake that appears to be of epic proportions (Rev. 11:13), wherein a tenth part of the city of Jerusalem will just plain "collapse" and 7,000 people will be killed, leaving the survivors "terrified" and "giving glory to the God of heaven" (Rev. 11:13b). With this event loud voices shouting from heaven:

> The kingdom of this world has become the kingdom of our Lord and of his Messiah, and he will reign for ever and ever" (Rev. 11:15b).

Earth's finest hour had now finally come! Then it will be that our Lord will grasp his power and his rightful authority as he begins his reign over all nations and all the universe and all creatures (Rev. 11:17). With that the temple in heaven will be opened and there will be seen the Ark of his Covenant (Rev. 11:19). After so many had cried out so often, "How long, O Lord," this will be one very satisfying and extremely spectacular work of God. This finale to earth's history will be greater than any Super Bowl football game or the reenactment of D-day, for it will exceed any conceivable previous awesome event on Planet Earth.

Is it any wonder, then, that we find all that is so central and dear to us as Believers in the work God did in the life of Elijah? Elijah truly was and still is the forerunner of our Lord and his awesome glory. As James told us, Elijah is more than rightfully held forth as a model of effective prayer (James 5:12). He also functions easily as one of the *sine qua non* examples of a faithful witness to the gospel and the person of our Lord Jesus (Yeshua) the Messiah.

Conclusions

1. Prayer obviously was the secret of Elijah's power. That is how James 5:12
2. presents it. This surely is a guideline for us in our day as well.
3. John the Immerser shared the Spirt and power that Elijah possessed (Luke 1:17). This could be seen in John's short ministry of six months in the word.
4. The discussion that took place on the Mount of Transfiguration was both encouraging and strengthening to Yeshua. Moses had a special contribution and Elijah had another, but both will be part of the soon to happen event of providing our redemption.
5. The two witnesses of the Revelation 11:3-19 again feature Moses and Elijah. God began his gift of revelation by giving his word and he will conclude it in that final day the same way.

Questions for Discussion and Reflection

1. In what ways do Moses and Elijah summarize the entirety of the *Tanakh*'s revelation of God's word?
2. How would you explain what Yeshua meant be saying that Elijah had both already come and that he will come yet in a future day? Does this involve a contradiction in terms or an enigma?
3. Why do you think our Lord limited the number of disciples to the three that he took up on the Mount of Transfiguration? Why these three?
4. Why do the enemies of God hate in such a fierce way the teachings of the two witnesses? How does this same spirit find itself in our own culture and times?
5. Why does our Lord allow the two witnesses to lie in the streets of Jerusalem for three and a half days?

Introduction to
The Prophet Elisha

The intense atmosphere in northern Israel was ominous and just as sultry as the weather. There was more than just a slight hint that some dreadful thunderstorm or calamity was hanging over the heads of the Israelites. In fact, from every side threatening clouds rose from the horizon of the land as the boom and clap of the thunder perhaps already could be heard in the distance. For a long time now, the patience of God's mercy over the land had held off the threat of any total disaster to the ten tribes up north, but with little or no repentance on the part of the nation which stubbornly insisted on walking contrary to the will of God, it was no longer a threat; it was a reality that was going to come! The fall of Samaria in 721 B.C.E. was not that far away!

Prior to the arrival of this son of the farmer in Abel-Meholah, the prophet Elijah had ministered patiently and fervently for some twenty years. However, his efforts had yielded very little change or repentance, given the likes of the apostate dynasty of King Ahab (I Kings 17-21). Nevertheless, Elisha's mentor and predecessor had withstood the opposition of the palace in Samaria almost single-handedly as he continued to declare the word of God.

Now it was Elisha's turn to call the nation to repentance after his great mentor had been called home to heaven in a whirlwind. Moreover, King Ahab, by the judgment of God, had been slain in the battle of Ramoth-Gilead and his son Ahaziah had succeeded him, but only for a brief time. This brevity was caused by his sending messengers to the god of Philistia, Baal-Zebub, to see if he would recover from his fall through the second story palace lattice. Despite a prophetic rebuke, there was no indication of any national repentance.

The crown of the ten northern tribes passed on to Ahaziah's brother named Jehoram, the second son of King Ahab and Queen Jezebel. Thus, it happened, that the prophet Elisha began his ministry in Jehoram's reign. While Jehoram did not rack up the record for evil exactly comparable to his brother or father, nevertheless he did no evil in the sight of the Lord. One would think that given the miracles he had seen in the life of his father and brother, Jehoram would have wised up and smelled the coffee. He did remove the image of Baal that his father had installed, but he retained the calves his father had set up at Bethel and Dan. He also connived with his mother Jezebel in some of her vile practices. Therefore, the cloud of God's judgment did not seem to move very far from the northern ten tribes during his reign.

However, Elisha was both an evangelist and a forerunner of Yeshua. Elisha would lead back to the Lord any and all who would be aroused by the impending judgment which hung over their heads. For those who became aware that they, as the northern ten tribes (as well as the two southern tribes) were facing judgment, God gave deliverance and the joy that comes from heeding his word.

The power of the word of God would rescue all who would believe and heed the teaching of the word of God from this servant.

Lesson 8

Rescuing a Nation
From National Disaster

2 Kings 2:1-14

The Prophet Elisha

At this time, Israel as a nation was on the slippery slope morally, ethically, religiously and in every other measurable way. She needed help, but where could that help be found now that she had turned away from God. As for God, he would send one man, for in Biblical math, one person plus God always constituted a clear and overwhelming majority. While this one prophet, Elisha, ministered, the threatened judgment might be delayed, or averted altogether, due to the preaching of God's word, It all depended on the response of the people!

Previously, there had been the man Elijah, who had been mightily used of God, but he now had been removed from the scene and had been translated directly to heaven in a whirlwind. However, before he had been translated to glory, he had cast his mantle on a farm boy from up in northern Israel named Elisha. His father, Shaphat, owned twelve yoke of oxen, used for plowing and cultivating the land. Elisha, we assume, must have been among those 7,000 Israelites who had not bowed the knee to Baal. Indeed, the very name Elisha meant "My God is Salvation" or "the God of Salvation."

Elisha had three marked characteristics. First, he showed no discontentment with his present calling in life as a plow boy on his father's farm. Second, he was ready to fulfill his duty, no matter how humble the calling, until God directed him to some other task. But when God called, through God's servant Elijah tossing his mantle on his shoulders, he was just as ready to move ahead in obedience to God's call. Can we assume that his father Shaphat and Elisha had attended the giant meeting at Mount Carmel, when Elijah had called down fire from heaven? They certainly could have been among that crowd.

Nevertheless, when the prophet Elijah showed up at their farm, and signaled the fact that God had called this young man, he had been more than prepared to leave his father, for he immediately followed his mentor Elijah before God took that leader from this earth.

The third characteristic of this young man was that Elisha was willing to follow God's call all the way, as previously stated, for he cut off all possibilities of returning to the farm, when he used the wooden plow he was handling in the field as fuel for the fire, and the team of oxen that pulled his plow, as the meat for the celebration of his new call for service.

Text: 2 Kings 2:1-14

Title or Subject of the Lesson: Rescuing A Nation From National Disaster

Focal Point: V. 14, "Then [Elisha] Took The Cloak That Had Fallen From [Elijah] And Struck The Water With It. 'Where Now Is The Lord, The God Of Elijah?'"

Homiletical Keyword: Ways

Interrogative: What? (Are The Ways To Rescue A Nation From National Disaster?)

Memory Verse: See V. 14 Above In Focal Point)

Outline

I. By Training Those Who Will Lead In The Future – 2:1-8

VIII. By Recruiting Those Who Value Spiritual Power -2:9-10

IX. By Challenging Those Who Will Stand In The Gap – 2:11-12

X. By Demonstrating The Power Of God – 2:13-25

The Lesson

By Training Those Who Will Lead In The Future – 2:1-8

A Theophany

Elisha already sensed that God was about to do something extraordinary through his mentor, for he steadfastly refused to leave the side of his trainer Elijah. Repeatedly, Elijah encouraged his younger companion to "Stay/remain here; the LORD has sent me to Bethel or Jericho or the Jordan" (2, 4, 6), but Elisha was just as adamant; he would not leave Elijah's side. Elisha stated in no uncertain terms, "As surely as the LORD lives and as you live, I will not leave you" (2b, 4b, 6b). So, in each case, the two men continued on together down towards the Jordan River.

The Scripture does inform us in verse 1 that "The LORD was about to take Elijah up to heaven in a whirlwind." Such whirlwinds were often connected with storms that heralded a divine self-revelation of God in a theophany, i.e., an appearance of God (cf. Job 38:1; 40:6; Ezek. 1:4; Zech 9:14). Therefore, God would manifest himself in the midst of this stormy whirlwind. It would be a disclosure of the presence and power of God.

This would be Elijah's last day on earth, but he had not disclosed this fact to his young understudy Elisha. But it seems, however, that Elisha must have known about this fact, perhaps by means of a separate revelation that was given to him. Certainly, there was knowledge that something of this sort was going to happen, for the "sons of the prophets" in the schools at Bethel, Jericho, and the one near the Jordan River, also knew that something was up, for they followed the two men at a distance.

The two men walked along, perhaps in silence, as their minds may have been filled with the events of the days earlier in their ministry during those last few years when they had served together. Perhaps Elijah's mind went back to those early days of his childhood as he grew up in Gilead, east and north of the Sea of Galilee, and Elisha may have been remembering his early days with his father Shaphat on the farm in northern Israel at Abel-Meholah. So, they may have exchanged some reminiscing conversation as they walked together (11a).

Elijah may have been testing Elisha, it would appear, when he ordered Elisha to "Stay here!" But a better surmise would be that he wanted him to stay behind because of his humility. He may have wanted his translation to heaven not to be witnessed by anyone if it was not the will of God and if it would mean some type of magnification of his person as someone special, rather than God himself. The credit and honor was to be God's alone, not his servant Elijah's. But in fact, God had in some way also revealed this magnificent coming event simultaneously to the sons of the prophets and presumably to Elisha to establish their calling and his with this magnificent and miraculous seal on the life and ministry of his servant Elijah. It would be a confirmation that ADONAI was God of gods, Lord of lords and King of kings! He could show himself to be strong on behalf of those who loved and served him.

How could this not affect these men? Such an event as this, where a mortal had been taken directly from earth into heaven without passing through death, had not happened since the days of Enoch, the seventh important person from Adam, who also had been taken directly into heaven in his mortal body. Only one other man had ever gone directly to heaven without going through the experience of death. This experience would be a special episode for those who would face a lot of opposition in the days ahead as "sons/schools of the prophets."

In the Schools of The Sons of the Prophets

It should not be surprising that the schools of the prophets were established in the very cities where the chief seats of false religion and gross idol worship had also been set up. Certainly this was especially true of the city of Bethel, where King Jeroboam had set up one of two calves as the object and place where Israel should worship (1 Kings 12:29). Gilgal must have been the city so named that was southwest of Shiloh, not the one near the Jordan River.

Both Bethel and Gilgal are named by the prophet Amos (4:4), and by the prophet Hosea (4:15), as centers of false worship. With some tongue in cheek, Amos said ironically, "Go on ahead and go to Bethel and Gilgal and sin." But Hosea warned in a more straightforward way. "Don't go to Bethel and Gilgal to sacrifice." In fact, he called "Bethel," meaning "the house of God," by the name of "BethAven," meaning the "house of iniquity." Nothing is noted about Jericho, but it too was no substitute for Jerusalem, or its temple for the worship of God. God would send his prophet right to the centers and the heart from where evil was emanating.

Elijah wanted to visit the three "seminaries" he previously had had a major hand in developing for just this one more time before his departure to glory. No doubt, Elijah's motive in wanting to visit was to strengthen and to fortify the lives of his disciples, for he had some idea of how hard the pressure was going to be in the years to come. Thus, he could consecrate them for the work he had begun and which his associate Elisha would continue. Elijah, like the apostle Paul, had fought a good fight and he had kept the faith (2 Tim. 4:7-8). He too, like his Lord, Yeshua, had loved his own,

who were in the world, for he had loved them to the end (John
13:1). So typical of Elijah, he had dedicated himself to serving and
encouraging his disciples to carry on in his absence, for they must
now know how to function without his presence.

The men from these schools followed the movement of Elijah
and Elisha very closely on that day of Elijah's departure. Even
though they stood at a distance (7), they did see how Elijah "took
his cloak, rolled it up and struck the water with it:" (8a). When
Elijah did so, the water of the Jordan "divided to the right and to
the left, and the two of them crossed over on dry ground." (8b).
This was the work of God!

By Recruiting Those Who Value Spiritual Power –
2:9-10

A Request for a "Double Portion" of Elijah's Spirit

After the two men had crossed over the dried-up Jordan
River, Elijah wanted to know "What can I do for you before I am
taken from you?" (9). Interestingly enough, Elisha did not ask for
greatness, fame, or riches; nor did he ask for power, nor nobility!
Instead, he coveted earnestly the best gift, which in this case was
a double measure of Elijah's spirit (9c). It must be noted, as a side
light, that John the Immerser came in "the Spirit and the power of
Elijah" (Luke 1:17). No, Elisha was not asking for the ability to
do twice the number of miracles as his predecessor had done, nor
was he asking for twice the effectiveness as an evangelist as Elijah
had demonstrated in his lifetime. No, his request was based on
Deuteronomy 21:17, where the "double portion" is represented as
that which the oldest, the firstborn son, received a double share of
the inheritance of the family. The text in Deuteronomy 21:17 reads:

> [The father] must acknowledge the son of his unloved wife as
> the firstborn by giving him a double share on all he has. That
> son is the first sign of his father's strength. The right of the
> firstborn belongs to him.

Requesting a Difficult Favor

Elijah confessed that Elisha had asked for a difficult request for him to grant; however, he put the fulfillment of this request on a condition that would be under the control of God. It would not depend on Elijah's will, or on the mere wish and request of Elisha; God would have to grant this request.

Apparently, Elisha was requesting that in light of the great needs of his day, and his own assessment of his own small gifts and powers, that God might grant from heaven above what would be similar or even more vividly seen than the gift Elijah had manifested? The condition was this: "If you see me when I am taken from you, it will be yours – otherwise not" (10b).

Can we name some of these gifts that Elisha was requesting? Yes! There was a Spirit of faith, one that rested in the presence and power of God. There was also the Spirit of obedience, one that sought always to do God's will. There also was the Spirit of raw courage that was willing to stand up against all the odds of that day and count on the fact that one person plus God always made a majority. These, perhaps, were some of the gifts Elisha requested.

By Challenging Those Who Will Stand in the Gap – 2:11-12

Persons Who Stand in the Gap

Psalm 106:21-23 remembered a time when Israel had exchanged their glory for an image of a bull-calf at the time when Moses was up on Mount Sinai and the people demanded a god from his brother, Aaron. In response, he made the golden calf. But the Psalmist says that God would have destroyed the Israelites, "Had not Moses, his chosen one, stood in the breach/gap before him to keep his wrath from destroying them" (Ps. 106:19-23; Exod. 32:7-14). That same call for a person to stand in the gap can be seen in Ezekiel 22:30, where the Lord says:

I looked for a man among them who would build up the wall and stand before me in the gap on behalf of the land, so I would not have to destroy it, but I found none.

Elijah had been just such a man, for during his days, he had stood in the breach/gap, when others had chosen to walk contrary to the will of the Lord. Now, however, he was about to be removed from this earthly scene. What would happen?

The Nation's Best Military Defense Against All Opponents

As the two prophets were walking along talking to each other, suddenly a "chariot of fire, and horses of fire, appeared and separated the two men." (11a). Elisha saw what was happening and so he cried out: "My father! The chariots and horsemen of Israel" (12). Then Elisha saw Elijah no more (12b). Elisha took hold of his own clothes and ripped them apart in his grief over his sudden loss of his mentor and friend (12c). The work would now belong to Elisha alone.

Elijah had served as Elisha's spiritual father. Together they had served in the ministry of the word of God. But now Elijah had been removed dramatically and suddenly in a whirlwind, leaving Elisha to cry in despair: "There goes the best defense this country ever had," he said in effect, for Elijah was better than a huge number of chariots and horsemen defending the country of Israel.

Back in 1854, Henry Blunt stated this fact best of all. He declared:

> Elisha, therefore, knew what alas, few [Believers] ever dream of knowing, that the devout and holy followers of God, are the support and safeguard of their country …. The real strength of our beloved country exists not in her fleets, her armies, her wealth, or even in her free and invaluable institutions, and the high intellectual endowments of her senators, but simply and entirely in the blessings of her God! And this will rest upon her in proportion as her governors are holy and God-fearing men, and her inhabitants are religiously-instructed and a praying

people. These are the "chariots of Israel and the horsemen thereof" (Henry Blunt. *Lectures on the History of Abraham, Jacob and Elisha.* Philadelphia, H. Hooker, 1854, p. 217).

Thus, the chariots of fire and the horsemen of fire are symbolic representatives of the strong defense Elijah had personally been to the kingdom of Israel for all those years he had spiritually ministered to his people (just as it will also be said later on of Elisha at the time of his death, 2 Kings 13:14). Accordingly, we may say the same for all of God's faithful messengers and laypersons who dare to stand in the gap between the living God and a godless generation and a sensate culture. Their worth and value exceeds that of all the latest nuclear weaponry, its drone airplanes, and latest gadgetry in military hardware that a country can create or own.

This is not a form of civil religion that says, "My country, right or wrong." It is to say what Proverbs 14:34 says:

Righteousness exalts a nation,
But sin is a disgrace to any people.

All of this warning about a possible future judgment was not what contemporary thought scornfully calls "Tanakh vengeance," but it is to say that when a culture or people become tone-deaf to the claims of revelation in Scripture and shut their ears to the message of the word of God, then God will speak through the events of times – perhaps through famines, earthquakes, drought, tornadoes, massive wild fires, or the like. There is a maudlin sentimentalism that repudiates all forms of divine punitive action and the rights of justice, truth, and ethical norms that are dependent on the character of God, but God will not withhold his judgment forever and tolerate injustice, wrongs, sin, and falsehoods to go on unabated, for they go against his very nature and character. So, there is a payday someday. Either repentance or judgment must come!

By Demonstrating the Power of God – 2:13-25

Accrediting Elisha and Looking for Translated Elijah -2:13-18

Now that God had taken Elijah directly into heaven without dying, Elisha's question was: "Where now is the LORD, the God of Elijah?" Elisha was now on his own, but he wanted the same presence and power he had seen God render to Elijah to be placed on his own life. God answered the prayer of Elisha in three great acts: (1) the miracle that imitated Elijah's striking the water with his mantle (13-18), (2) the healing of the water of Jericho (19-22), and (3) his announcing judgment on the forty-two jeering kids from Bethel (23-25).

Elisha's first miracle came as evidence that his petition had been heard and his office as a prophet of ADONAI had been vindicated. Elisha had taken the cloak that had fallen off of Elijah as he was translated to heaven, and he used it to strike the water as his mentor had done. When he struck the water, it too divided to the right and to the left, so he was able to cross over the Jordan River on dry land as he had come over that same way with Elijah (13-14). The company of the prophets then knew without a doubt that "the spirit of Elijah [was now resting] on Elisha" (15a). God had vindicated Elisha as a true messenger of his word and acts. "Where now is the Lord God of Elijah?" He was right there with his servant Elisha!

The sons of the prophets were, however, uncertain about what had happened to Elijah, despite their revelations of his translation to heaven to the contrary. They begged Elisha to let them go searching for Elijah until finally he was embarrassed by their constant begging (16). They searched for three days, thinking perhaps that the storm and the whirlwind had dropped him on some remote mountain or in a ravine, but they were unable to find any trace of Elijah (18). When they returned empty-handed, Elisha rebuked them, saying, "Didn't I tell you not to go." (18b).

How much are we today like those from the schools of the prophets? They knew what God had said he was going to do, yet they insisted perhaps there was a catch to it or that something had gone wrong! How many times does God need to communicate his word before we actually act on the basis of that word?

Healing the Water of Jericho – 2:19-22

Jericho had previously been under a divine curse, for as Joshua finished destroying Jericho in Israel's conquest of the land, he uttered a curse on it (Josh. 6:26).

> At that time Joshua pronounced this solemn oath: "Cursed before the LORD is man who undertakes to rebuild this city, Jericho. At the cost of his firstborn son will he lay its foundations; at the cost of his youngest will he set up its gates."

In the days of King Ahab, Hiel of Bethel defied this curse and laid the foundations of Jericho, but it cost him his firstborn son, Abiram, as God had promised through Joshua (1 Kings 16:34). He also lost his youngest son, Segub, when he set up the gates of Jericho, in accordance with the word of the LORD spoken by Joshua son of Nun. Therefore, it might also have been true that the curse was likewise upon the ground and its water supply connected to Joshua's curse! The water, therefore, was notoriously bad!

In a half hour walk from the city of Jericho, there is a spring called "The Fountain of the Sultan" (Ain es Sultan). It rises from the base of a hill that looks like an Indian mound today, but has a strong, steady supply of cool, sweet water. But in Elisha's day the water was "bad" (19). Elisha asked that "new bowl" be brought to him with salt in it (20). Elisha then went out to the spring and threw the salt into the water as he said, "This is what the LORD says, 'I have healed this water. Never again will it cause death or make the land unproductive'" (21). And so, it happened, and it has remained that way to this day according to the word Elisha had spoken (22).

This whole act was a prophetic symbolic action in which the visible signs of a new bowl and the salt only represented what God was about to do. The bowl had to be new, so nothing done previously with that bowl was to be connected with the miracle seen here. Neither the bowl, the salt, nor even the preaching could bear any proportion to the healing that was done here, for it was enough for the word of God to say, "I have healed these waters." God can render any means effectual, or he can do the same miraculous works without means, or even by the most contradictory of means.

Judgment on FortyTwo Kids From Bethel Who Jeered Elisha -2:23-25

The third event that validated the new call of Elisha was found in vv. 23-25. At first, we are put off by this story that sounds so unworthy of such a great prophet. Perhaps the prophet should have overlooked the jeering of these forty-two kids, but the issue here was more than a mere slighting or offending of a new prophet; in their act of mockingly yelling at him to "Go up," "Go up," they were taking a deliberate swipe at the miraculous work of God in translating Elisha's predecessor to heaven in a whirlwind. Their jeers should have been rendered: "Blast off, Blast off, baldhead;" go to where your predecessor disappeared and leave us alone, they apparently yelled!

These youths were not innocent babies or small kids, but they were those who were older, perhaps in the teens or even older. We conjecture that they heard the discussions of their parents around the dinner tables in Bethel that denied, or that openly mocked, the idea that Elijah had been caught up to heaven. Thus, the children picked up the chant and mockingly called Elisha, who was still a relatively young man himself, to get out of their lives. "Baldhead," was a mark of disgrace and dishonor in that culture. But to ridicule God's servants was to demean God himself (cf. 1 Cor. 3:16-17). Herein lay the danger in this situation.

Elisha did not lose his temper, as some assert, but instead he called on God to vindicate his own name and reputation. Elisha merely announced what God had previously warned about in his word as stated in Leviticus 26:21-22—

> If you remain hostile to me and refuse to listen to me ... I will send wild animals against you and they will rob you of your children.

This was a judgment designed to wake up the people, lest a worse disaster befall them. A loving God warns and pleads from his word before his wrath descends on such blasphemous youths as were found in Bethel. But if there was not any repentance, then that whole generation would eventually be swept into captivity, because of their abominable sins (cf. 2 Chron. 36:16). God would rather change us by our responding to his word than use the events of life to startle us into a full reality check to call us to a repentance before him.

Conclusions

1. Where do you and I put our strongest emphases on the defense of our country? Is it in the smarts of our leaders and in the sophistication of our military hardware, or even the seize of the national military budget, or is it in our dependence on God, his word, and our holy living?

2. What is your deepest request from God? Is it to obtain in life a certain kind of fame, an honor, or some major recognition, or is it in obtaining a double portion of the Spirit of God?

3. What will the family, our congregation, or nation say of us when we die? Will they too say, as they did for Elijah and Elisha, "There goes the best defense our nation ever had?" Their way of life, their prayers for this nation and their teaching of God's word were beyond and in excess of any military hardware we possess or could even hope for. Or will their estimate of us be different?

4. What training do you seek to be better prepared to serve the Lord? Do you think schools of the prophets or the like are still needed today? Has biblical illiteracy and the poverty of Bible knowledge been raised to an unacceptable level?

5. God will certify his own servants by fulfilling the word they speak on behalf of heaven or in bringing judgment on those who mock and reject the God they announce to their generation.

Questions for Thought and Reflection

1. To what degree should the Church or ministry depend on a trained group of men and women?

2. How responsible are we who are just lay persons responsible to study God's word for ourselves in addition to what we are taught by God's servants?

3. How could one or two prophets be the best defense a nation could possess; indeed one that was of greater effect than all of the military hardware or software that nation possessed?

4. On the current scene, can you think of anyone in our day what might fulfill the exact role attributed to Elijah and Elisha with regard to defending our nation?

Lesson 9

Confronting the Secular Spirit of the Times

2 Kings 3:1-27

The Prophet Elisha

The scene in 1 Kings 3 marks a change into a time of war and battle. But it also became the occasion for three kings to experience deep embarrassment as well as a time when all three kings had to go to the prophet Elisha to ask how they could extricate themselves from the mess they had managed to get into in the first place.

The king of Israel, Joram, a.k.a. Jehoram, the son of King Ahab and Queen Jezebel, "Did evil in the eyes of the LORD, but not [to the degree that] his father and mother had done" (2). He did get "rid of the sacred stone of Baal that his father had made" (2b), but he "clung" to the worship of the calves King Jeroboam had set up as the gods that had delivered them out of Egypt (3).

Now King Mesha of Moab decided to rebel against King Joram, in order to get relief from his annual tax assessment of 100,000 lambs and the wool of 100,000 rams, which he had to supply to Joram each year. Moab was a pagan country on the southern boundary of Joram's kingdom, which had been subjected to Israel ever since King David had conquered them and announced "Moab is my washbasin" (Ps. 60:8; 108:9), as they had ever since struggled to throw off this yoke. Yet God would use the rebellion of Moab as a means to chastise King Jehoram/Joram, who had likewise drifted away from ADONAI.

Instead of negotiating with King Mesha, or inquiring of God whether he should undertake such a battle, the king mobilized all Israel (6) and set out from Samaria with his troops. He sent a message to King Jehoshaphat, king of Judah, and asked if he would go with him to fight against Moab (7), to which Jehoshaphat replied in his characteristic style of acting first and thinking later, "I will go with you, I am as you are, my people as your people, my horses as your horses" (7c). Jehoshaphat was a great joiner, yet he was always more than a bit naive, but one, nevertheless, who wanted to follow God and do what was right.

When asked what route they should take to attack Moab, Joram suggested the novel route of coming in from the desert of Edom (8). So the two kings set out for battle through the wilderness of Edom, and when they reached Edom, whose king was also a tributary of Jehoshaphat, and who had a governor appointed by Judah (1 Kings 22:48), he too joined them to form a troika of kings and a combined army to attack Moab. Edom, at this time,. These three allies flattered themselves that with such a huge number of such forces, they felt they could be victorious over Moab; however, they trusted entirely on the arm of flesh. They had badly miscalculated this route and its challenges, for despite such an imposing force of three armies linked together, they were not as invincible as they thought. After they had advanced some seven days into their march, the heat of the desert became intolerable, and the supply of water suddenly dried up in every direction (9). Now, weak, dejected, and languishing from lack of water, they were in real danger of perishing in a most miserable death.

When King Jehoshaphat of Judah asked if a prophet of ADONAI was present (11), one of the officers of Joram replied that "Elisha son of Shaphat [was with them, who] used to pour water on the hands of Elijah" (11c). Jehoshaphat noted correctly that "the word of the LORD is with him" (12a), so these three kings humbly went to seek his counsel in the prophet's own quarters, not in theirs (12b). Therein lies the setting for our lesson.

Text: 2 Kings 3:1-27

Focal Point: V. 13 "Elisha Said To The King Of Israel, 'What Do We Have To Do With Each Other? Go To The Prophets Of Your Father And Mother.'"

Title Or Subject Of The Lesson: "Confronting The Secular Spirit Of The Times"

Homiletical Keyword: Times

Interrogative: When? (Do The Times Arise When We Must Confront The Secular Spirit Of Our Day?)

Memory Verse: Same As Focal Point In V 13

The Outline:

I. When We Become Unequally Yoked With The Unrighteous 3:1-9

XI. When We Call On God Only In Our Emergencies -3:10-15 A

XII. When We Fail To Act On The Basis Of God's Word – 3:15b – 27

The Lesson

When We Become Unequally Yoked With the Unrighteous -3:1-9

We Must Seek First the Living God and His Kingdom -3:1-3

Ahab's son Ahaziah had died after a mere two year's reign as a result of his falling through the palace lattice from the second floor

(2 Kings 1). He had scornfully and wickedly sent messengers to the god Baal Zebub in Ekron to see if he would recover from his fall and his resulting injuries. But as Elijah had predicted, he soon died from his injuries.

Now his brother, Joram, was named the next king. Surely he had witnessed a tremendous amount of times where the prophetic word of God had proven to be truthful and thoroughly believable over against the pitiful showing of the prophets of Baal and Asherah; but instead, he too "did evil in the eyes of the LORD" (2 Kings 3:2). He had missed the ethical norm for all moral acting, which was to act in accord with what was right in the eyes of the Lord. He had, it is true, shown at least some scattered tokens of following the Lord by his getting rid of the sacred stone of Baal (2c; cf. 2 Kings 10:26-27), but he was addicted to the northern penchant for worshiping these bull-calves, which Jeroboam had set up. But the point remained: No one can serve God and mammon at the same time, nor can believers be united with unbelievers in such ventures (2 Cor. 6:15-17). If we are to be holy as the Lord is holy, then it will call for times when we must separate ourselves from the times and culture we live in.

We Must Not Lean on the Arm of Flesh to Deliver Us 3:4-9

We must always remember that God alone is the arranger of times, seasons, boundaries, and destines. King Joram thought that an imposing presence of a trinity of kings and their armies would be unbeatable. However, God had other plans, for they ran out of water in what might have been considered otherwise to be a brilliant move by attacking Moab from their blind side. Now these three kings were in danger of being destroyed!

Then, all of sudden, the once high and mighty King Jehoram cried out in his desperation, "Has the LORD called us three kings together only to hand us over to Moab?" (10). In fact, this is what David had sung many years ago before this event in Psalm 18:26:

To the pure you show yourself pure,
But to the crooked you show yourself shrewd.

It had not occurred to Joram that God could have been moving against him alone, and not against Jehoshaphat. It seems almost to be a rule, that when the wicked get into trouble, they love to have the righteous for scapegoats. It is even possible to see how mortals often change their views on religion when they get into such difficulties when they are unable to extricate themselves from such danger.

The point was that after marching the three armies roundabout for seven days through the hot desert (9b), the army had no water for themselves, or for their animals (9c). Jehoram had come to the end of his rope and had it not been for the presence of King Jehoshaphat, there would have been no directions or incentive from God on how to extricate any of them from the hole Israel had dug for themselves and the other two kings and their armies. It was time to heed the word of God.

When We Call oOn God Only in Emergencies – 3:10-15a

Be Thankful for a Righteous Remnant –

If King Jehoshaphat had not been there (14), Elisha would not have respected godless Joram and his request. But that also raised another question: What was Jehoshaphat doing there in the first place? It would seem that this was a case where occasionally good men make common cause with bad men, for which they only have themselves to blame in the event that tragedy or unanticipated calamity comes from the venture. But this was so characteristic of King Jehoshaphat, for he had fallen into the same trap with Joram's father, Ahab, when he gave the same answer to an invitation to go up to reconquer Ramoth-Gilead (1 Kings 22:4c). He was one slow learner, but fortunately he was always quick to repent and to confess his sin of not seeking the will of God before he joined in such a venture.

Be Grateful for Those in Whom the Word of God Dwells

Joram's parents, Ahab and Jezebel, and his brother Ahaziah, had despised Elisha's predecessor, the prophet Elijah and his message, so what made Joram think that he would now listen to the word of God from Elisha? This also raises another question: Why was Elisha also marching with these three armies? Was it that God knew what end this venture would result in, so our Lord had Elisha join ranks and go along for the sake of his servant Jehoshaphat? For, as far as we are able to reconstruct, the events that had followed Elisha's experience at the Jordan River when Elijah was taken into heaven, he had taken the road from the Jordan up to Bethel, where a bunch of forty-two nasty hooligans mocked him. After this he seemed to have retreated to Mount Carmel for solitude and meditation. If our guess is correct, from there he rose, strengthened and fortified for the ministry ahead. God must have directed him to return to Samaria, where he found the army about to march against Moab. That seems to be how Elisha found himself among this troika of kings and armies.

When the kings learned that Elisha was in their midst, the three kings went to visit him, rather than summoning Elisha to come to their own private council chambers (12b). In so doing, they showed respect for the prophet and for the word of God he represented. It does not seem that Elisha was embarrassed, or even surprised by their visit, for God must have told him long ago that this is how things would come to a head. And even though Joram was apostate and backslidden, he knew that ADONAI alone was God, for when he was told to go and inquire of the prophets of his father and mother, he responded with a clear negative, "No!" (13c). He knew deep in his own experience by now that it was no use asking these dead-head prophets, for he had heard how miserably these false prophets failed on Mount Carmel and how their Baals had failed his sick brother, when only God knew what would happen. God's word was with Elisha and his word was the powerful and truthful word of God.

When We Fail to Act on the Basis of God's Word – 3:15b-27

The Importance of Music

Music may have been taught and practiced at the schools of the prophets, for the first thing that Elisha asked for when he was seeking a revelation from God was a "harpist" (15a). It must have been a means of drawing his mind and the soul away from the world about them, and thus a way of allowing it to dwell on divine things.

Martin Luther said: "One of the finest and noblest gifts of God is music. This is very hostile to Satan, and with it we may drive off many temptations and evil thoughts." He went on to say,

> After theology, I give next place and highest honors to music .... It has often aroused me, so that I have won a desire to preach .... We ought not ordain young men to the office of preacher if they have not trained themselves and practiced [singing] in the schools.

Well said, indeed! Let's put it into practice!

It might be asked how in the desert of Edom they found a harpist, but it might also be that some of the army members brought along some of their musical instruments. Actually, we can only guess at this matter, for the text does not inform us otherwise.

The Importance of Obedience to God's Commands

It was while the harpist was playing his instrument that the word of the Lord came to Elisha. They were to "make this valley full of ditches" (16). That must have startled those kings as it did the armies, for what good were ditches out in the middle of a desert of sand? How would that do any good, especially digging these trenches in the suffocating heat they were experiencing?

Nevertheless, what other options did these three kings have? Even though there were no clouds in the sky, or any signs whatsoever of any rain, they were to dig these ditches by faith, thus making provision for what as yet had been unseen! The reason they were to do so was because the Lord had said, "You will see neither wind, nor rain, yet this valley will be filled with water, and you, your cattle and your other animals will drink" (17). And if that seemed to be something that appeared to be too easy for God to do (when it actually did not look at all possible), God would also do the harder thing by handing over Moab to them (18). These three armies would overthrow every fortified city and every major town (19). They were to cut down every good tree and stop up every spring and throw the stones all over every good field (19b-c).

The way all this happened was on the next morning, after all the ditches had been dug the day before and perhaps the evening before - at about the time of the morning sacrifice, God would send rain that would fall in the country of Edom, a great distance from the ground where the three kings were camped, i.e., in the eastern hills of Edom. Water would flow from these hills and fill the ditches in the valleys of Vadi el Kurahy and Vadi el Ahsy where the armies had labored to provide dry ditches in the sand (20). Thus, this rainfall happened while the people were at prayer in the early morning watch, presumably after digging all afternoon and all night.

Some many wonder why God chose so indirect a method? Why not just simply preserve the army in the first place. But had God delivered them more directly, the three kings and their troops. may have been tempted to attribute this victory to their own prowess. Moreover, King Jehoshaphat would have had one less warning about his propensity to join anything in order to be accepted. Also

King Joram would not have seen and experienced the power and rebuke of God as dramatically as he did in this manner.

The point is this: God not only gave water, he also gave the victory. By this time, the Moabites had heard that the kings were coming (21a), and therefore they had mobilized every man, young or old, who could bear arms, and stationed them on the borders to their land (21b). But as the sun rose that fateful morning for them, the water looked red like blood in the glow of the morning sunrise (22), for they had no knowledge, nor was it possible for any water to be out in the valley in front of them anyway. They assumed the red color was "blood" (23a), and that the three kings had fought each other and polished each other off (23b). So the word went out: everyone to the plunder (23c).

However, when the Moabites came out to the site where Israel had camped, the Israelites rose up and fought them so hard that they routed them completely (24). The battle was carried then to the towns of Moab. The land of Moab was invaded, the Moabites were slaughtered, the fields were covered with stones, the springs were stopped up and every good tree was cut down. The only town that survived with its stones in place was Kir Hareseth (25), but the part of the army that was armed with slings surrounded that capital city and attacked it as well.

The Moabites worshiped their idols, which became a snare to them. Moreover, they sacrificed their sons and their daughters to demons. They shed innocent blood, the blood of their sons and daughters, whom they sacrificed to the idols of Canaan, and the land was desecrated by their blood. They defiled themselves by what they did; by their deeds they prostituted themselves.

Even though they did not deserve it, God was gracious to Jehoshaphat and to Joram, as he showed his mercy to them just as he does to us. But these kings had to learn the lesson the hard way except for the goodness of God.

Conclusions

1. If it be asked again, "Where now is the God of Elijah?" the answer is that he can be found in the midst of the trials of life showing his grace and mercy and to his new servant Elisha.
2. Instead of adopting a secular Geist or worldly cultural outlook on life, we need a renewed spiritual mind-set that sees God's working in all the events of life.
3. We must be careful of forming too quickly alliances with those who do not love the Lord, for they can often lead us into trouble.
4. Be grateful for the powerful presence and the power of the word of God.
5. Do not become unequally yoked with unbelievers, for what fellowship can we have with such alliances?

Questions for Reflection and Thought

1. How important in your thinking and planning for Church worship is the ministry of music?
2. How responsible are the people of God for the atrocities that take place as the defeat of wickedness rages with the obvious outcomes that occur to pagan?
3. What are the proper and improper boundaries for defining when we must separate ourselves from non-Biblical types of alliances and when we must cooperate with others in various projects?
4. When we act on our own and therefore get into trouble, as Jehoshaphat did, may we expect God will always provide a way of escape in all these instances?
5. How does a believer develop a godly mindset and avoid being conformed to the pattern of this world?

Lesson 10

Helping Those Who Seem
To Be Beyond All Help

2 Kings 4:1-44

The Prophet Elisha

The phrase "culture of death" has been appropriately used in our day as a catchphrase for those who favor abortion and euthanasia. The mention of a "culture of death" conjures up names like the American case of Roe vs. Wade in 1973, when abortion became legal in the USA, the case of Terry Schiavo, who was allowed to starve to death under professional care, or the macabre sale of human organs by Planned Parenthood that often operates in a clandestine manner in our society.

The culture of death, however, operated a long time ago during the times of the Omride dynasty, when death and dead idols permeated the society, especially under King Ahab and Queen Jezebel and their descendants, Ahaziah and Joram. All of this flourished just when God wanted the people to experience new life and productivity under his blessing, but the people were resolute in their opposition to God's rule over them. Thus, they perpetuated the culture of death in their day as well.

Text: 2 Kings 4:1-44

Focal Point: V. 43, "How Can I Set [These Twenty Barley Loaves] Before A Hundred Men?" His Servant Asked. But Elisha Answered, "Give It To The People To Eat. For This Is What The Lord Says: "They Will Eat And Have Some Left Over."

Title or Subject of the Lesson: "Helping Those Who Seem To Be Beyond All Help"

Homiletical Keyword: Gifts

Interrogative: What? (Are The Gifts That God Will Give To Those Who Appear To Be Beyond All Help?).

Memory Verse: V. 43 As In Focal Point

The Outline:

I.   Our Gift Of Relief From Distress – 4:1-7

XIII. Our Gift Of Life Twice Over4:8-37

XIV. Our Gift Of The Power Over Death – 4:38-41

XV.   Our Gift Of Multiplication Of Little Into Much – 4:42-44

The Lesson:

Our Gift of Relief From Distress – 4:1-7

The miracles that Elisha used from God to good effect in chapters 4:1-6:7 were done for private individuals or for the sons of the prophets, but those that were described in chapters 6:8-7:20 were miracles that bore more on political circumstances of the nation, and the king as leader of the nation.

The fourth chapter of 2 Kings, however, demonstrated four types of need that were accompanied with four types of responses from the prophet, wherein the four responses formed an inclusion as seen in the following chart:

Types of Need:	Types of Responses:
v. 2 The Destitute	Multiplication
v. 13 The Rich	Restoration
v. 40 The Harmful/Poisonous	Restoration
v. 43 The Deprived/Shortages	Multiplication

For Those Who Fear God

The narrative begins with the wife of one of the "sons of the prophets," who came to the prophet Elisha for help. The place where this incident occurred is not mentioned, for it could have been either at Gilgal, Jericho, or Bethel (1 Sam. 10:8-10). She told her desperate story to the prophet of how her husband, who had revered the Lord, and who had apparently had been enrolled in this school of the prophets headed up by the prophet Elisha, but who had suddenly died in what may have been an early unexpected death (1b). Now the creditor of the deceased was pestering this widow woman to pay up what her husband had owed them (1c) –- perhaps some of the money he had used to pay for his own tuition or living expenses at the school of the prophets? This creditor was now demanding from his widow the last possession she had on earth – her two boys (1c). This importune creditor was now seeking immediate relief from his debt by requiring the boys to render seven years of service, as the Torah provided for (Deut. 15:1).

The Jewish historian Josephus and some rabbis claimed that this widow's husband was the same Obadiah who was Ahab's secretary of state (1 Kings 18:3ff), since he too "feared God." But that is a slim basis on which to make an identification between the two men. Both "feared" or "revered" God, but that was the end of the similarities.

For Those Who Possess Nothing

To get relief from this predatory creditor, the woman cried out to Elisha. When he asked how he could help her (2), he further inquired, "What do you have in your house?" (2b). She replied that she had "nothing at all, except a little oil" (2c). Elisha's instructions were that she should "Go around and ask all [her] neighbors for empty jars" (3a). She was not to ask just for a few, but for many. Once she had done this, she was to "Go inside and shut the door behind [her] and [her] sons" (4a). Then she was to "Pour oil into all the jars, and as each [was] filled, [she was to] put it to one side" (4b).

This widow knew the extent of her calamity, of course, but she did not yet know the full extent of God's love and mercy for her and her two boys. Her estimate of what she now owned was "nothing!" The little bit of oil in her estimation counted for nothing. However, when she said that she owned nothing, she showed she was totally aware of her inadequacies and thereby she became a ripe candidate for the grace of God – one who was fully dependent on outside help, since she had little to nothing to offer to assist in what was going to happen.

So it came about, that as long as one vessel still remained empty, the multiplication of the oil did not cease to flow until the whole supply of empty vessels was filled. God's riches, as seen in the flow of the oil, in his infinite grace was close to being inexhaustible. All too many men and women, in such a situation, try working harder, but they often end up harvesting less unless God chooses to send his blessing from above (Hag. 1:6). In place of all such human effort, 2 Chronicles 16:9 says that "The eyes of the LORD go to and fro throughout the whole earth to show himself strong on behalf of those who love him." It is not appropriate, either, to teach in this situation that the oil is a type of the Holy Spirit, for the woman will be instructed to sell the oil, which would not be appropriate way to treat the blessed Holy Spirit.

So, what indeed did happen? When she reported to the man of God all that had taken place in her life and that all the empty jars were now filled, he told her to go and sell them, and pay her debts, but she and her sons could live on what was left over after the debt was paid (7). God's grace and mercy triumphed over death! God had provided, but it took the obedience of her acting on the basis of faith before the jugs would be filled.

Elisha, like his master Elijah, helped a widow in her desperate circumstances by a miracle of multiplication (cf. I Kings 17:8-16). Now, in the next incident, he would also help by raising a child back to life again, just as his predecessor had also experienced (2 Kings 4:29-37; cf. 1 Kings 17:17-24).

The Gift of Life Twice Over – 4:8-37

For Unrecognized Needs

The prophet Elisha returned to Shunem, where lived a "well-to-do-woman" (or as it is in Hebrew, "a lady of prominence, dignity, social distinction, a women of valor," Prov. 31:10ff.). But this Shunamite woman too had a problem, as real as the destitute widow in vv. 1-7, for which Elisha's God also had a solution. She offered the man of God a meal whenever he came by their city (8b), but she had additional plans as well, for she discussed a plan she had conceived with her husband.

She sensed that Elisha was a "holy man of God" (9), so she wanted to make a small room for Elisha on their flat roof that would include a bed, a table, a chair and a lamp (which may be where Holiday Inn first got their room decor from!? v 10). This would make a place where Elisha could stay whenever he came to minister nearby. Surely, she exhibited the gift of hospitality, just as later the New Testament would remind us in Hebrews 13:2,

"Remember to entertain strangers." Her provisions were at the same time the provisions of a loving Heavenly Father.

It was just on one such occasion, when Elisha and his servant Gehazi stopped by the Shunamite's house, and her newly prepared prophet's chamber, that Elisha expressed his appreciation for all that this well-to-do- women had done for him. As a result, he asked his servant to summon the Shunem woman to their newly prepared room (12). When she arrived, she stood in the doorway before Elisha as he asked her, "Tell me, you have gone to all this trouble for us. Now what can be done for you? Can we speak on your behalf to the king or the commander of the army?" (13).

Her response was, "I have a home among my own people" (13c), meaning "I am content and I don't need anything, thank you!" (15). Elisha still was not satisfied, so after she apparently had left them, he continued to discuss the matter with this servant, Gehazi: "What can be done for her?" (14a). His servant observed, "Well, she has no son and her husband is old" (14b). That was the idea that Elisha liked.

It would appear that the prophet had already laid the matter out before the Lord and had obtained an answer along these lines. So the Shunamite woman was summoned once again and she came and once again stood in the doorway. Elisha boldly announced to her, "About this time next year, you will hold a son in your arms" (16a). But she protested, "No, my lord, don't mislead your servant, O man of God" (16b). She did not want to be prematurely excited or to arouse any false hopes, for she had probably lived with the realization that this was something that was impossible for them as a couple. Even though she had not entertained the prophet for any sake of gain or reward, but for the sake of serving her Lord, God would graciously fill her unspoken and perhaps her unrecognized need for a son and a future companion when her older husband perhaps later passed on to glory.

For Recognized Needs Such as Sunstroke

But to her surprise and perhaps to the delight of both of them, she became pregnant according to the promise of God in that next year (17). The boy grew up and God was good to them, but one day the young boy went out into the fields where his father was working with the harvesters when he suddenly complained that his head was hurting him – possibly from a sunstroke (18). Typical of a man, the father told one of the workers to carry the boy immediately to his mother (18c). However, the sick boy sat on his mother's lap until noon, and then he died while she was still holding him (20b). Tragedy had struck – perhaps as she had feared it would!

She took the boy's corpse up the outside stairs to the prophet's chamber on the flat roof and put him on the bed where Elisha usually slept, shutting the door as she left (21). Without alerting her husband or anyone else as to what had happened, she called to her husband and asked him to send one of his servants with a donkey so she could go quickly to the man of God (22). Her husband thought this was a strange request, since it was neither a new moon nor a Sabbath, when his wife ordinarily went to the prophet (perhaps for a local Bible study), but he nevertheless agreed (23). So she and the servant set out for Mount Carmel, which was a dozen or more miles away (24).

When Elisha saw the woman from Shunem some distance away, he realized something must be wrong, so he asked his servant to run and inquire of her if everything was all right. Was something wrong with her husband? Was her child all right? (26). Undeterred, she hastened on, without stopping to answer the questions Gehazi was supposed to get answers to. She fell at Elisha's feet, from where Gehazi tried to push her away (27), but Elisha restrained Gehazi. "Leave her alone!" he said, "She is in bitter distress, but the LORD has hidden it from me and has not told me why" (27c). Then the woman poured out her heart and Elisha realized it was all about her son (28). He had died!

Elisha instructed Gehazi to get ready to run quickly, without greeting anyone along the way, and go to the woman's home, carrying the prophet's staff in his hand (29). He was to lay the staff on the boy's face (29c). But the mother's instinct was sharper than most realized, for she knew Gehazi was not the man for the job, for she must have picked up something that was amiss in his service for God. She insisted on Elisha himself going to minister to her son (30). Her reasoning must have been something like this: If he by the power of God could provide her a son when she and her husband were as good as dead, then surely this same prophet could bring that boy's life back to him again! So Elisha got up and followed her back to her village in Shunem (30b).

Meanwhile, Gehazi had gone on ahead, as Elisha had ordered and had placed the staff of the prophet on the boy's face (31a), but there was no response. So Gehazi retraced his steps as he intercepted Elisha and the boy's mother, saying, "The boy has not awakened!" (31c). Certainly, this shows that the staff alone was merely a symbol of divine power, but it was in and of itself powerless to do anything apart from God himself! If there was any virtue to come from the staff, it could not be invested in the staff itself, but it would come from the energy given to the man who held that staff, which energy came from the prayer of faith and trust in the promise of God. This women must have guessed that Elisha's servant did not have the right stuff, so that is why she insisted that Elisha had to come, even though it was a four to six hour trip to Shunem from Mount Carmel! Among other things, Gehazi lacked a sympathetic heart, as can be seen when he attempt to push the woman away from the prophet. Since he lacked that, along with whatever else was a problem in his life, Elisha's staff was no more than a common stick in his hands!

Moreover, it is impossible to do the work of God by proxy, as if the job can be pushed off onto someone else – e.g., in our day such tasks are often pushed off on perhaps a parent, a Christian school, a Sunday School teacher, or something of that sort. However, God's work has to be done in God's way, but it cannot be done by proxy!

When Elisha reached the house and his prophet's chamber, where the boy was lying on his bed (32), he shut the door on the two of them (33) and he prayed to the Lord (33c). Then he got on the bed and lay on the boy, mouth to mouth, eyes to eyes, hands to hands, as the boy's body grew warm from his lying on him (34). Then the prophet arose and walked about the room and then resumed his position over the boy's body once again. Finally the boy sneezed seven times (35).

It was time to share the good news with the lady of the house, so Gehazi was instructed to summon her (36). When she came, he said, "Take your son" (36c). She immediately fell at Elisha's feet and bowed to the ground and then she took her son and left the room (37). God had worked a miracle and the woman knew it was from God! Her son was given to her now for second time by the power of God!

The Gift of the Power Over Death – 4:38-41

In Spite of the Apparent Insignificance of the Incident

The prophet Haggai had instructed the people of his day not to despise the day of small things (Hag. 2:1-10). In a similar way, Elisha had gone to Gilgal during a time of famine in the land, to meet with the company of the prophets (38a-b). While there, he had instructed his servant Gehazi, "Put on a large pot and cook some stew for these men" (38c),

One of the prophets went out in the fields to gather herbs and came across a wild vine (39a). Not knowing exactly what he was dealing with, he gathered enough gourds to fill the fold of his cloak. When he returned, he proceeded to cut up the gourds and to add them to the stew that was now cooking (39 b). These gourds seemed to be something like wild cucumbers, known as *cucumis colocynthi*, a poisonous creeping vine, that has light green leaves and a very bitter round yellow fruit about the size of an orange. It could produce the colic and give violent purging effects.

In Spite of the Unlikeliness of the Means Employed

Previously when Moses had encountered bitter waters, he had been told by God to toss a piece of wood to relieve the bitterness, and also in another earlier event, Elisha had purged the water near Jericho by tossing in salt, but in this case as the men began to eat the stew, they cried out in pain, "O man of God, there is death in the pot! And they could not eat it" (40).

Elisha ordered that they get some flour and put in the pot, then it would be all right for the sons of the prophets to eat (41). Once again, the restoration was greater than the means employed, for flour has no known powers such as these men witnessed. It did not depend on the flour, but on the power and blessing of God, which far surpasses even death. Thus a mere handful of flour in the hands of the Almighty was more than enough to disarm the throes of death and disappoint the grave of one hundred potential victims.

The school of the prophets did not hesitate to eat the stew, for faith did not hesitate, nor was it ashamed now. Though this was but a small event to a few in a school at Gilgal, it too was linked to even more glorious events in God's final triumph in the last day.

The Gift of Multiplication of Little Into Much – 4:42-44

The Gift of Firstfruits

In what might have been the first evidence of a godly man from Northern Israel, who rejected calf-worship that was then so dominate in the ten tribes, a man from Baal-Shalishah chose instead to bring his offering of his first fruits to the school of the prophets as his substitute place for the worship of God (42). The twenty loaves he brought were from his first pickings out of the new barley harvest, as specified in Numbers 18:13 and Deuteronomy 18:4. These prime pickings, from the first of the harvest, were to be offered to the Lord and then he in turn relinquished them to the priests and the Levites. Here, however, they were given to the sons of the prophets in recognition of God's work being done by them.

A Gift With Great Potential

When Elisha ordered that these twenty loaves of barley bread be set before the 100 prophets in Gilgal, Gehazi, ever the rationalist, naturally objected (43), for he could see that the twenty loaves would not go very far with one hundred hungry sons of the prophets eating from them. Nevertheless, Elisha continued to order that Gehazi should not give up his task, for God had a special word about this situation: "They will eat and have some left over" (43c). Thus, just as God multiplied the oil in the first incident in this chapter, so he once more multiplied. In both cases there was a surplus! This multiplication would not only be enlarged, but exceedingly replicated, in Yeshua' miracles of multiplying the loaves and the fishes on the shores of Galilee, with a large amount of left-overs. The lesson was clear: we should not be anxious or worried about such things, for God cares for us just as he cared for one hundred prophets from the school at Gilgal.

Conclusions

1. The staffs in our hands, the flour in the pot of stew, the amount of oil left in a jug, and the few loaves to feed so many, bear little or no direct relationship to the impact or the nature of the spiritual results that come as miraculous gifts from God.

2. Let us allow God to gift each of us so we too may have the joy of dispersing the blessing and honor of God around the globe.

3. Never doubt in the dark times of a crisis what God has shown us in better times when we were walking in the light.

4. God is able to take the first pickings of all we earn, to make, and to extend them exceedingly abundantly beyond what we might ever even have imagined to his honor and glory, when we offer them to the Lord.

Questions for Discussion or Reflection

1. Why do the same means, when used by some not work, but
   when used by others, work: such as the prophet's staff in the
   hands of Gehazi, as opposed to Elisha's use of the same staff?
2. Why are we asked not to worry about whether the gift is large
   enough to match the enormity of the needs when we give that
   gift?
3. Why did God give a son to the Shunammite woman and allow
   death to take that same son?
4. Why did the prophet's widow have to go through all the
   trouble of filling those vessels with oil and sell them, when
   Elisha could have just produced the money she needed right
   then and there?

Lesson 11

Extending the Gospel Mission to the Gentiles

2 Kings 5:1-27

The Prophet Elisha

When Believers think of our Lord's missionary challenge to take the good news into all the world, they generally go to the Great Commission in the end of Matthew's or Mark's Gospel. But here in the Tanakh is a wonderful narrative of how a young captive girl's testimony was used by God to introduce a foreign Gentile Captain to the God above all other gods. Some have placed the emphasis of this chapter on baptism, but that does not seem to be the point of this narrative.

From the very beginning of the story of the Bible, there was a promise of an inclusion of Gentiles in the family of God by means of Abraham's seed. This came to a climax in Genesis 12:3, "In your seed all the families of the earth will be blessed." But Naaman was not the first Gentile to be blessed in this manner, for it seemed as if at every major juncture in history of Israel, a Gentile appears as a convert to be numbered among the covenant people. One cannot help but recalling the Gentile priest and king, Melchizedek, who met Abraham as he returned victorious from rescuing Lot (Gen. 14:17-29), nor the throng of the "mixed multitude" of Egyptians that left their home country when the Israelites left that the land of their captivity (Exod 12:38). The Gentile priest Jethro likewise shared a fellowship meal in the worship with Moses in the desert of Midian (Exod 18:13-27) and the Canaanite Rahab of Jericho became a new convert as the city was being conquered by the Israelites (Josh 2:1-21). King Hiram of Tyre also gave willing assistance to Solomon in the building of the Temple of ADONAI (1 Kings 5), so the story continued through the Tanakh. In our chapter of 2 Kings 5, the grace of God extended beyond the borders of Israel as the leader and victorious general of the Syrian army, Naaman, came under the influence of Elisha's ministry because he had become afflicted with leprosy.

Leprosy in the Tanakh is not necessarily what we today know as Hanson's Disease, the modern form of leprosy, where limbs rot and fall off. Instead, it seems in this period to be something more like psoriasis with its symptoms of flaking skin, and discoloration of body hair, and the exposure of flesh through the skin (Deut. 13). It was more of a social, than physical, disability. It is a disease that would have disqualified Naaman, had he been planning on going into the presence of God in the Temple if had thought of living in Israel, but thanks be to God, he was not only cleansed from his disease in this chapter, he was freed to go directly to God in prayer and worship as a cleansed and renewed man who was now part of the people of God.

Text: 2 Kings 5:1-27

Title or Subject of the Lesson: "Extending The Gospel Mission To The Gentiles"

Focal Point: "Naaman and all his attendants went back to the man of God. He stood before him and said, 'Now I know that there is no God in all the world except in Israel.....'"

Homiletical Keyword: Areas

Interrogative: What? (are the areas where the good news was extended to a Gentile such as Naaman?).

Memory Verse: V 15 as in focal point

The Outline:

The Lesson:

It Extended to All Classes – 5:1-3

Including Captive Maids

There was much that a little girl could have been bitter and resentful about, for after all, she had been captured in a raid on her homeland of Israel and had been carted off to a foreign people and the land of Syria/Aram. Her new master was Naaman, the commander and chief of the army in Aram/Syria. One can only imagine her heartbreak and tearful longing to be restored to her parents back home, for this was one of the evil results of war.

However, there was also much to be amazed at, despite the tragedy of her situation. In the providence of God, she had fallen into the hands of none less than the wife of the commander of all the armies of Syria (2). It is also amazing that she had been given the grace of God to speak apparently without reproach even to her enemies of how her new owner could have relief and a cure from his disease of leprosy (3). By so doing, she had something that was even greater than her freedom. Her God was the God of the whole earth and he could work his grace in the lives of Gentile Syrians as well as Jewish Israelites.

So she uttered a wish in sheer simplicity: "If only my master would see the prophet who is in Samaria! He would cure him of his leprosy." (3b). Her faith was strong, for as far as she was concerned, God's prophets had power to cure even such loathsome diseases as Naaman's leprosy.

Including People in Positions of Power

Naaman is described as being a man who was "a great man" in the sight of his king, but he was also seen as one who was "well-formed" or "beautiful," but now disfigured by this troublesome disease of leprosy(1). One minute we see him decorated with all sorts of ribbons and laurels from the battlefield and in the next as one tormented with the symbol of worriment. He was also called a "valiant soldier," or a "mighty warrior" (1d).

Moreover, ADONAI had given to him victory over the armies of Israel! (1c), which demonstrated, once again, that the LORD was Lord over all history and all nations (Amos 9:7); the same Lord who had granted Assyria the power to win over her enemies (Isa. 10:5), or even for Babylon to win over her enemies (Hab. 1:5-11). This same message would later be given by the Lord to Sennacherib, king of Assyria in 2 Kings 19: 25-26), when he said, "Have you [Sennacherib] not heard? Long ago I ordained it. In days of old I planned it; now I have brought it to pass, that you have turned fortified cities into piles of stone...." God was indeed Lord over all history and all nations.

It Extended to All Situations – 5:4-14

Including International Incidents

When Naaman heard this good news from his captive Israelite maiden, he immediately went to the king of Syria and asked if he would send a letter of introduction for him to go to the king of the people he had been conquering to see if he could be healed by their prophet. Talk about *chutzpah*, this was about as nervy and as brazen as one could get. Naaman had beat up on the nation Israel, but now he would elicit a favor from their king! However, the king agreed to send such a letter, because he wanted his commander–in-chief to be healed. It must have been a social embarrassment for the king to have to keep his general in the background at state functions because of this social liability and the appearance of his skin.

The Syrian letter to the king of Israel simply read: "With this letter I am sending my servant Naaman to you so you may cure him of his leprosy" (6b). You can imagine what the king of Israel thought about such a request: These Syrians must have the nerve of brass monkeys! He complained, who do they think I am:

"[Am I] God?" Can I kill and bring back to life? Why does this fellow send someone to me to be cured of his leprosy? See how he is trying to pick a quarrel with me!" (7b-c).

Naaman left his country and set out for Israel hoping to be cured. However, he also incorrectly thought God's miracle of grace could be purchased, for he took along ten talents of silver, six thousand shekels of gold and ten sets of clothing! If a talent is 750 pounds and we value silver today somewhere around $30.00 an ounce, then the value of this gift would be around $360,000. If a shekel is about 150 pounds, and we value gold at somewhere near $1,400 an ounce, then the value of this gift in current terms would be about $3,360,000. Finally, depending on what was included in the ten sets of clothing, but let us set it around a middle priced suit and shirt and accessories at $300 each, this would equal another $3,000. The grand total of the gifts he was going to offer would amount to a staggering $3,363,360. This general and king wanted Naaman to be healed in the worse way, to say the least! Forget about the amount of shekels it would take!

Elisha the prophet heard about the distress of the Israelite king and that the king had torn his robes in grief (8), so he sent the king a message: "Why have you torn your robes? Have the man come to me and he will know that there is a prophet in Israel." The question arises, however, why didn't the king of Israel know this fact and immediately think of the prophet Elisha? Did this event not expose the fact that the king of Israel himself had not availed himself of the resources God could have supplied him time and again? So the king sent him to where Elisha lived and Naaman stopped at his front door (8c).

Including Offended Pride

Elisha sent a messenger to the door when Naaman arrived with his chariot retinue. The Syrian general expected more from the prophet, like a quick miraculous healing. However, Elisha did not even bother to come out and greet him. He simply sent this message:

> Go, wash yourself seven times in the Jordan, and your flesh will be restored and you will be cleansed (10).

That really angered and teed-off Naaman to no ends, for he felt such treatment was way below his pay grade. He had expected him to come out and then, as he stood in front of him, wave his hands over the spot of his disease, and call on the name of ADONAI, with the result that he would be healed (11). But no! Instead, he had told him to go dip in the Jordan River seven times, the muddiest of all rivers, for the two rivers in his city of Damascus, in the capital of his own country, the Abana and Pharpar, were much better and clearer than the waters of this Jordan River (12), so he turned and went off in a rage. That prophet, he must have thought, is trying to make a fool of me!

But what Naaman did not realize was the fact that his healing was to be from such an unlikely means that God alone would receive the glory, not any special water, with or without mud, nor any special prophet. But this was all too much for this proud general. He now felt he had been made of fool of and had been on a wild goose chase; it all was just a lot of nonsense.

But Naaman's anger was risky and dangerous, for this anger almost turned him away from the cure he so desperately sought. He had such a high opinion of his own judgment that he (as sometimes we too exhibit) had the temerity to think that he knew how this ought to be done. He had counted on his rank and position as something that would get him better treatment, for he was now trying to measure the divine standard by his own earthly conceits and opinions. But his preconceived notion about how this would be done for him was not the only cause for his displeasure. He also did not like the remedy God had sent through the prophet to him. Why the muddy Jordan River and not some other? And the answer to that question, of course, is that none of the other remedies he was thinking about had the divine promise of healing attached to them. He did not realize that God can take the lowliest of means used and turn them into the most blessed of results, and that was just because of the character of the One who stands behind that word! So, we should never judge a river by its color and don't judge the work of God by its seeming appearances, for if we are going to be helped by God, we must be disabused of our proud delusions.

Naaman's servants, however, served him well, for they came up with a lot of good sense. They argued with their master this way: "If the prophet had told you to do some great thing, would you not have done it? How much more, then, when he tells you, 'Wash and be cleansed'" (13). The logic and the thinking was priceless. That was exactly what Naaman needed to hear. With that bit of wisdom, Naaman was somewhat persuaded to give it all a try (14a), for when he did, "his flesh was restored and became clean like that of a young boy" (14b). Can you imagine how he complained after each of the first six times he dipped in the muddy water with no evidence of any change! His servants must have been on pins and needles for giving him the advice they had offered. But then on the seventh dip, he appeared and the astonishment on all faces in that small crowd would have been worth several selfie photos to send home!

It Extended to All Lands – 5:15-19a

Regardless of the Nationality

Can you imagine the surprise and the joy on Naaman's face when he realized that he was totally healed? He went back to the prophet's house and boldly declared:

> Now I know that there is no God in all the world except in Israel. Please accept now a gift from your servant. (15b)

He was thrilled! Naaman's confession sounded much like Acts 4:12 where the apostle Peter taught: "There is no other name under heaven given to men whereby we must be saved," for this was not just a cerebral knowledge, for when he used the word that he now "knew" there was no other God in all the world, this use of the word "know," as many of these usages in the Tanakh demonstrated, was a personal knowledge of the Lord that he now affirmed.

Elisha quickly declined to accept any Naaman's gifts, expensive or not, for he did not even wish him to get a small hint that Naaman's gifts were in some measure commensurate with the miracle of his healing. It was all of grace and not a bit of it was from works. So, all payments were graciously, but firmly refused.

Regardless of the Localities of the Worship of Adonai

To demonstrate that he was most sincere about his new intentions to worship the God of Israel alone, Naaman requested that he be allowed to take back home as much dirt from Israel as two mules could carry (17a). This, of course, was a very peculiar and strange request, but it seems he wanted to worship ADONAI, whom he had just seen work of his behalf and whom he now knew was superior to any other god; in fact ADONAI had no rivals at all! But his request should not cast doubt on the evangelical nature of his confession in v. 15. His purpose in making such a request was not to set up an idolatrous image, nor to become another heathen symbol, but to literally be on good "grounds" as he offered sacrifices and offerings to ADONAI. He had no intention of keeping his confession in ADONAI a secret. Let everyone in Syria know ADONAI was God alone!

Interestingly enough, Elisha does not forbid Naaman to adopt the priestly office, nor does he rebuke him for asking such a question, but for this new believer in an isolated and heathen land, Elisha seems to grant him permission to take greater liberties than Deuteronomy provided for. In that sense, then, Naaman is an early anticipation of the Gospel Era. He pointed to the fact that the fences on the ceremonial law would be removed as the office previously held by the priests and Levites would ultimately spread to all the people in every nation (cf. Mal. 1:11).

Krummacher said it best when he observed:

> Should we suppose that he associated with it any superstitious notion, such a surmise would only show our inability to estimate and comprehend some of the more refined and nobler natural feelings of the human soul... [as] a mere leaf from a tree ... on the mount of Olives .... [or] a few wildflowers ..... [from] the Garden of Gethsemane ..... [so] a few bushels of dirt....could not, in physical properties be at all superior to that of Damascus [dirt], yet with [Naaman] it was dirt from the land which the Lord had distinguished [himself] above all lands...It was dirt from the memorable place where this delighted stranger had experienced inestimable benefit, where he had found the living God, and in him eternal life. (F. W. Krummacher, *Elisha: A Prophet For Our Times*, Grand Rapids: Baker Book House, 1976, 204 -205)

The fact that he found pleasure in possessing this dirt, which brought back to him sweet recollections, should not trouble us and lead us to ridicule him, for these were innocent feelings that had been awakened in a new believer who was still rejoicing in the work God had done.

Naaman also asked for ADONAI's forgiveness when he had to accompany his king on his arm as they went into the temple of the idolatrous Rimmon and he bowed together with his master (18). Elisha did not debate the issue with him at this time, for he merely said, "Shalom" (19a). That was enough for the moment!

It Extended to All Pretenders – 5:19b-27

Beware of the Love of Money and Things

Naaman left the prophet's home, but before he had gone very far, Elisha's servant Gehazi felt he was getting off too easy, especially in light of the needs they had at their schools of the prophets (20-21). So he ran after him with a farfetched story that Elisha had sent him to say that "Two young men had just come to [the school of the prophets] from the hill country of Ephraim [presumably a poorer part of the country]. Please give them a talent of silver and two sets of clothing" (22). But he had done all of this on his own and without the permission or authorization of Elisha.

Beware of Hypocrisy

Gehazi had served Elisha for some ten to fifteen years by now, so he knew the language and the garb of what sounded right. But he was clearly out of order in what he did, despite the wonderful motive that led him to do it. When Gehazi returned from this mission of raising funds, Elisha asked him where he had been, but Gehazi professed not to have gone anywhere. However, Elisha was with him in spirit, even when Naaman got down from his chariot and gave Gehazi the money and garments (26). As a result, Elisha said Naaman's leprosy would cling to Gehazi and his descendants forever as a judgment from God (27).

Was this punishment too harsh, especially when Gehazi had done it all supposedly with a good intentions? No, said Keil in his commentary on this passage:

> It was not too harsh a punishment that the leprosy taken from Naaman on account of his faith in the living God, should pass to Gehazi on account of his departure from the true God. For it was not [Gehazi's] avarice only that was to be punished, but the abuse of the prophet's name… and his misrepresentation of the prophet. (C. F. Keil, *Biblical Commentary on the Old Testament: The Book of the Kings*, transl. James Martin, Grand Rapids: Eerdmans, 1950, 322-323)

Grotius on Acts 5:2 commented: "he who seeks to deceive the prophet in relation to the things which belong to his office is said to lie to the Holy Ghost, whose instrument the prophets are."

Conclusions

1. We must once more see that even in the Tanakh the extent of the Gospel was intended to be for the whole world.

2. We need to labor without ceasing to see that the whole world has a chance to recognize this great Lord and to claim him as their Savior.

3. We need to constantly monitor ourselves to see if there is any phoniness in ourselves as we set our highest priorities on Messiah and his mission to preach the Gospel to every creature.

Questions for Discussion and Reflection

1. Does the Tanakh call for a mission to the Gentile nations?

2. Was the testimony of the captured Jewish maiden responsible for the salvation of Naaman in any way?

3. What other instances of a missionary mission to the Gentile can you cite from the Tanakh?

4. Did Elisha act properly in allowing Naaman to take home so Israelite dirt to use when he worshipped the Lord and to have a pass when he bowed down with his king to worship Rimmon?

Lesson 12

Heeding a More Sure
Word of Prophecy

2 Kings 6:1- 7:20

The Prophet Elisha

I t is difficult to know whether we should attach 2 Kings 6:1-23 to 2 Kings 5:19-27 in which we have three major attributes of our God (viz. his omnipresence [5:19-27], his omnipotence [6:1-7] and his omniscience [6:8-23]), or should we connect chapter 6 with chapter 7, since Elisha is sitting with the elders in his house in 6:32 and is still there in 7:1? We will choose the latter course of action since we have already covered chapter 5:19-27.

In fact, the story about Elisha making the ax head float can also, in some ways, be attached to 2 Kings 4:38-44, where the power from God is seen in the healing of death that was found in the cooking pot where the wild gourds were collected, as well as the multiplication of the twenty loaves with a good deal of bread left over. But let us take up the narratives in their Biblical order as presented in 2 Kings 6-7.

All too many interpreters have interpreted 6:1-7 *allegorically*, in which they have incorrectly said that the "iron" was a symbol of sin and the wooden "stick," that Elisha threw in at the spot where the iron sank, a symbol of peace and reconciliation or even a symbol of the wooden cross on which Christ suffered and died! Thus, Messiah died on a wooden cross, similar to the stick thrown in the water, to make sin powerless, when Messiah was likewise raised from the deep, where he had been buried. But this interpretation, ingenious as it may seem to be, misses the point that this was not any "iron" in general, but it was a definite implement, an ax head, one that was borrowed at that. So this attempted interpretation is altogether too wooden, if not a bit contrived!

Neither will a *naturalistic* interpretation do for this narrative, for this view has Elisha possessed of a quick "presence of mind," as he sharpened a stick, and then with excellent aim, hit the hole in the ax head so it could be lifted out of the water! However, this interpretation also fails to fit the context, for v. 6 does not mean to "sharpen," but to "chop off" a stick. Furthermore, the point of the narrative is not on Elisha's presence of mind, but the power of God. True, the prophet used physical means, but that is true of some other miraculous deeds as well.

Others inadequately try to use a *spiritualizing* method of interpreting this miracle by saying that the live branch was none other than Messiah, who went down into Jordan's waters for us, and he who was the Living One became dead in order to deliver us from the mire of sin. But there is nothing in the text that suggests any of these values; this is best taught in the New Testament text, but not here in this text. We must privilege the text in the Tanakh and give it our priority, not our thoughts or ingenious surmises taken prematurely from the New Testament and used to reinterpret or to retell the Tanakh story.

Instead, these miracles are given to us to lead us to certain conclusions that are valid and true, ones that come from our Lord himself. They are marvelous evidences of the power and wisdom of God, which work of God goes beyond our capacity to even imagine how such great gifts could come from so gracious a Lord.

Text: 2 Kings 6:1-7:20

Focal Point: 7:17 -18a, 20a, "Now the king had put the officer, on whose arm he leaned, in charge of the gate, and he died, just as the man of God had foretold when the king came down to his house. It happened as the man of God had said to the king …. And that is exactly what happened to him ….

Title Or Subject Of The Lesson: "Heeding a More Sure Word of Prophecy"

Homiletical Keyword: Outcomes

Interrogative: What? (are the outcomes of this more sure word of prophecy?)

Memory Verse: (Same As Focal Point Above)

The Outline

    I. God's Omnipotence Can Restore What We Borrowed -6:1-7

    II. God's Omniscience Can See What We Are Oblivious To -6:8-23

    III. God's Ending of a Famine Can Bring Us Back From Rebellion -6:24-33

    IV. God's Merciful Blessings Can Open the Windows of Heaven – 7:1-15

    V. God's Serious Warning to Those Disbelieving His Word -7:16-20

The Lesson

God's Omnipotence Can Restore What is Borrowed - 6:1-7

The School of The Prophets at Jericho Expands

The school by the Jordan River, presumably the one at Jericho, had by now expanded, it would seem, beyond the fifty men who had been present at Elijah's translation (note 4:43, where a total of 100 men had now gathered at Gilgal.). The work of God was growing and expanding, but the facilities had grown too small (6:1). So the suggestion was that each was to go down to the banks of the Jordan River, and after cutting down a tree, get a log that could be used to construct the expanded quarters for the school of the prophets (2). Elisha agreed with the plan, but then he was asked if he would go along with the men on their quest to fell the trees for lumber for the new quarters, to which he agreed (3). So off went the men and Elisha on their mission of cutting down trees for the anticipated construction of the enlarged quarters.

A Borrowed Axhead Flies Off the Handle

As one of the sons of the prophets was cutting down his tree, however, the ax head he was using flew off the handle and landed in the Jordan (5). This led to an outcry from him: "Oh my lord, it was borrowed" (5b). The economic impact of such a loss would be enormous for that student and for that school.

Elisha asked, "Where did it fall?" (6a). The bereft student showed the prophet the general place where the iron ax head fell. Elisha then chopped off a stick and threw it into the spot where the iron ax head was thought to have fallen (6b). The result was that he "made the iron float" (6c). The word the NIV translated "float," has been inappropriately rendered as "swim" in some versions, but it is more accurately rendered "overflow" in places such as Deuteronomy 11:4. But what took place definitely was a miracle, a direct work of God – the ax head was now on the surface where it could be seen.

The laws of nature, of course, obey the mechanisms set in them by their Creator, but God is also free to introduce his own supplementary or temporary provisions – or if necessary, to introduce temporarily a new creation, or a new law, just for this situation. So without suspending the laws of nature, our Lord intervenes through his prophet to introduce something new from his same creative power.

According to the law of the Land, the borrower was responsible to restore damaged (or even lost) property (see Exodus 22:14-15). Moreover, iron was a rather rare commodity in ancient Israel, so the loss of this item, as already noted, could have resulted in significant debt. If this member of the prophet's school was not able to restore this borrowed item, the lessor could have required him to enter "Debt slavery," until the full amount was paid back, or alternatively he could have been forgiven his debt. It was a serious moment for that man and this school.

Elisha's miracle was no small gesture of relief for that man, for he was delivered from a mighty debt when the ax head was recovered. Praise God for his miraculous intervention.

God's Omniscience Can See What We Are Oblivious To -6:8-23

God Sees and Knows Everything

God's omniscience is at one and the same time a characteristic that is both absolutely necessary to gain a right conception of God, and yet also one that is so difficult to understand. But it is simultaneously powerful and exceedingly influential when it is properly apprehended. Psalm 139:1-6 is perhaps one of the classic texts that sets forth this doctrine of omniscience best of all. Our Lord knows when we get up, or when we sit down; he knows even words before they are on our tongues: such knowledge, the Psalmist agreed, "is too wonderful for [him and for us]."

The events in this section of chapter 6 took place while King Joram, the son of Ahab, was king in Israel. In his days, the king of Aram/Syria was at war with Israel, but the thing that really upset the king of Syria was that after he had consulted with his officers on where he should set up his next camp, the king of Israel already knew exactly where that would be.

Here is how it happened: the man of God, Elisha, would send word to the king of Israel to avoid that spot, for the Syrian king was hiding in that spot to attack him (6:8b-9a). Thus the king of Syria was repeatedly frustrated in his plans to get the advantage over the king of Israel.

No matter where the Syrian king would decide to set up camp, which in Hebrew is delightfully called *peloni almoni*, meaning at "such and such" a place, or even more roughly: "what-cha-ma-call-it" site, or "wherever-it-was" (8c), the prophet Elisha would inform the Israelite king that the Syrians were camped at that spot. This so enraged the Syrian king that he thought his own military were leaking this information (11). But his men all firmly denied having any part in such a disclosure. Instead, they argued that it was Elisha the prophet who was tipping off the king of Israel, for Elisha knew the very words the king of Syria spoke even in his bedroom (12). It was not as if Elisha was clairvoyant, or that he was a gifted hacker into the Syrian king's intelligence system, or even one who tapped into an earthly or heavenly computer; no, he could see and know only what ADONAI had revealed to him. God could make Elisha aware of every word spoken by the king of Syria in his bedroom and in his secret councils, for did not our Lord know when and who the woman was who had touched him in the crowd (Mark 5:25-34)? Elisha was not guilty of some sort of foreign collusion; no, he had access to divine revelation!

The king of Aram ordered that Elisha be captured immediately, wherever he was. It turned out that he was at that time located in the city of Dothan, so the king of Aram sent horses and chariots to surround the city of Dothan by night (13-14).

The next morning when the servant of Elisha got up early in the day, he hurried back to Elisha with the shocking news that the city of Dothan was surrounded with horses and chariots of the Syrian army (15). Elisha reassured his servant that all was well by saying, "Don't be afraid; those who are with us are more than those who are with them" (16).

God Opens the Eyes of Those Who Are Spiritually Dull 6:17-23

Elisha prayed for his servant (as it must be true of us as well): "O Lord, open his eyes so he may see." This is exactly what the Lord did, for he opened the eyes of Elisha's servant so that his eyes saw what amazed him, for the hills were also filled with horses and chariots of fire all around Elisha (17b). Fire is the form God often used to signal his presence, and the horses and chariots were symbols of his protecting power as well (cf. 2:11). Earlier in Scripture, Jacob also was aware of such a squadron of a double army of angels when he thought he was threatened by his brother Esau (Gen. 32:2). The forces of our Lord are huge and are at the disposal of those whom he loves!

Often in our distress we cry out, "Oh, my Lord, what shall we do?" But our Deliverer is not far off. He gives his angels charge over us to keep us in all our ways (Ps. 91:11-12). In fact, the angel of the Lord encamps round about those that fear him (Ps. 34:7). So, why worry?

As the enemy came down from the hills toward Elisha, the prophet prayed to the Lord, "Strike these people with blindness" (18a), and that is what happened. Elisha then instructed these now blinded enemies, "This is not the road and this is not the city. Follow me and I will lead you to the man you are looking for" (19). So the man they were looking for was none other than the man Elisha who led them to Samaria, the capital of Israel, to the king of Israel himself.

God Then Opens The Eyes of the Blinded Enemy -7:20-25

What shall we say about Elisha's conduct? Did he tell an untruth? Can his conduct be excused on the basis that this was like any other military stratagem – i.e., it is OK to lie for the sake of a greater good? No, I do not believe so, for on the contrary, Elisha did not tell a lie, for his home was not in Dothan, but in Samaria. Moreover, Josephus, the Jewish historian, had it right when he said:

> Elisha asked them whom they had come to seek. When they answered: "the prophet Elisha," (where he was to be found) .... he certainly used a form of speech which the Syrians might understand otherwise than the way he meant it, but he did not pretend in the least to be anything else than what he was. That they did not know him was a divine dispensation, not the result of an untruth uttered by him.

We agree with this analysis!

A man, like Elisha, who saw the divine protection of horses and chariots of fire needed neither falsehood, deceit, nor a ruse in order to avoid capture or harm. The Syrians could see, but their perception of reality, from a divine perspective was definitely limited and greatly restricted. Only the Lord could open their eyes.

Once the enemy forces had entered the city of Samaria, the king of Israel, King Joram, wanted to know if Elisha would now order him to kill all of his enemies (21), but Elisha firmly replied: not at all. Captured men are not to be treated that way, so neither should these men (22); instead, the king was to set a big feast in front of them and after they were fed, then he was to release them and send them back home to Aram/Syria. Surely, that will be one difficult mission for the embarrassed Syrians to write in their annals, much less to tell to their friends!

As a result, the "bands of Aram stopped raiding Israel's territory" (23c). So the king of Israel had prepared, in effect, a table in the presence of his enemies (Ps. 23) and then he released them to go back home. Here was an army that had a real eye-opening experience! It would be one battle that would leave them scratching their heads – were we supposed to capture the prophet Elisha?

The Syrians had learned that it was impossible to fight against God. No one could outwit God or make moves that he was unaware of, or which he could not counter if he chose. Nothing could be concealed from the Lord. No one and nothing could compete with him? He was Lord and Sovereign over all.

God's Ending of a Famine Can Bring Us Back From Rebellion- 6:24-33

Disasters are Allowed by God for a Purpose –

Both Deuteronomy 26:29 and 28:52 made it clear that when Israel continued to be hostile towards the Lord, then all the curses that had pursued them would finally overtake them and the enemy would besiege them in all their cities. Thus it happened, that Ben-Hadad, after an interval of years, came once again to lay siege to Samaria (24), having learned nothing from the previous failures of that nation against Israel. I guess he assumed there was always one more new way that had not been tried before.

We Must Realize That Our Only Relief is From The Lord

The Syrian siege was most successful, for it lasted so long that a donkey's head or a dropping of a dove's dung sold for an inordinate amount of money (25). But as if that were not bad enough, the king heard a woman cry for help (about eating the son of the other woman as agreed previously; now the other woman had hidden her son when his turn to be eaten had come) as he passed by on the wall (26), to which he retorted, if the Lord does not help you, then where can I get help from? (27). The famine was intense and very severe! The people were left to cannibalism!

The problem, as already hinted at, was of course heart-wrenching. When the king inquired further as to what was the matter (28a), she described how the two women had agreed to eat her son today, and then on the morrow they would eat the other woman's son (28b). But when the morrow came, the other woman had hidden her son (29b), while they had already eaten the first woman's son (29a). When the king heard these gruesome details, he tore his robes (30a). As the king walked the walls of the city, the citizens saw he was wearing sackcloth under his clothes, a usual sign of repentance.

God is faithful to his word, both when we stubbornly refuse to repent and also when we do repent. So why had Israel been so slow to repent and turn back to the Lord? So enraged was the king that he took an oath to remove the head of Elisha from off his shoulders, for he concluded that this siege was the result of Elisha's pronouncing doom on the nation for its failure to live up to the calling God had given to them as a nation. He wanted to attack the messenger (i.e., Elisha) who had come with the warning news rather than confront the issues in the message!

Elisha, however, was seated in his own house in Samaria with the elders of the nation apparently gathered in conference around him (32a). The king was on his way to carry out his murderous threat to remove Elisha's head, when the king's own messenger, who had been sent ahead of him to carry out this fowl deed of his devising, arrived just ahead of the king who was hard on his heels (32b). Despite all that was going on in these tumultuous days, Elisha knew from God, not only what the king of Syria was up to, but also what the king of Israel was planning to do – whether it was going to be "heads" or tails! Accordingly, he told the elders, "Don't you see how this murderer is sending someone to cut off my head? Look here, when the messenger comes, shut the door and hold it shut against [him]. Is not the sound of his master's footsteps. behind him?" (32c-d).

While Elisha was still saying this, the messenger of death came with the king trailing behind him. His complaint was this: "This disaster is from the LORD. Why should I wait for the LORD any longer?" (33). Apparently Elisha had encouraged the king to hold out against the siege and wait for the Lord's deliverance, but King Jehoram/Joram had had enough. It is already clear that the king had donned the outward garments of repentance, with his sackcloth under his clothes, but he may not have been wearing them out of grief over his own sin and the sin of his people. In other words, he may have had "attrition," i.e., sorrow over the fact that he and his people had been *caught* in their acts of sinning, but he had no "contrition," i.e., godly sorrow for the actual acts of sin themselves.

To be sure, the delay in divine providence often tries the patience of the best of men, and ungodly men, like King Joram, say they are just not going to wait any longer. Elisha knew that King Jehoram was a son of the murderer Ahab, whose wife Jezebel slew many of the prophets of ADONAI. What more could one expect from a son from that kind of family? However, the Psalmist counseled, "I wait for the LORD, my soul waits, and in his word I put my hope. My soul waits for the LORD, more than the watchmen waits for the morning ..." (Ps. 130:5).

God's Merciful Blessings Can Open the Windows of Heaven -7:1-15

Wait for a More Sure Word of Prophecy

2 Peter 1:19-21 affirmed that there was real hope and a solid reason to wait for God's special word, for that word was most certain and more sure than any other word. Peter taught:

> We have the word of prophecy made more certain, and you do
> well to pay attention to it, as to a light shining in a dark place
> .... For prophecy never had its origin in the will of man, but
> men spoke from God as they were carried along by the Holy
> Spirit. (2 Pet. 1:19-21)

Elisha gave that sure and solid word of prophecy in 7:1. About this same time tomorrow, he promised, seven quarts of flour will be sold for a *shekel* (about 30 cents), and thirteen quarts of barley will go for the same price at the gate of Samaria (7:1c).

The king's chief officer, who was number three man in the king's three-man chariot, on whose arm he leaned, personally scoffed and expressed full doubt that such a thing could come about. "Why," he blustered, "Even if the LORD should open the flood gates of the heavens, this could [never] happen" (7:2). The prophet had spoken mere words; Samaria was under siege and attack, so who was going to make this possible, he reasoned. He, for one, was from Missouri, as the saying goes; he had "to see it to believe it!" But he would not live to see it in its entirety!

God Can Send a Panic to the Enemy

Our word "panic" is said to come from Greek mythology where the frightened god Pan accompanied the army of Bacchus, and who with a wild scream gave relief from an otherwise great enemy's danger. But in this text, there was no mythology; God sent relief by causing the Syrians to hear the noise of approaching chariots. Perhaps, it was thought it was a nation coming to Israel's aid and so they fled for their lives leaving all their stuff behind them (7:6-7). Suddenly there was food all over the place!

God Can Use the Most Unlikely Means: Four Lepers – 7:3-15

At the same time that this siege was taking place, there were four lepers who were hanging around the city gate of Samaria (4). They were trying to decide what to do, for as they figured it out, they had three options: (1) they could stay at the gate of the city where they had nothing to eat and then die, (2) they could try to enter the city, but they would only starve there also, for they had no money and the city was probably out of food anyway, or (3) they could go to the enemy and throw themselves on the mercy of the Syrians, for they were going to die anyway, so what was there to risk? (4). They decided that the third option was the best alternative of the three choices in front of them.

So the four lepers went to the camp of the Arameans at dusk, but to their astonishment, when they got to the camp, they found it totally deserted, "For the LORD had caused the Arameans to hear the sound of chariots and horses of a great army, so they said to one another, 'Look here, the king of Israel has hired the Hittite and Egyptian kings to attack us'" (6). Therefore the Syrians fled, leaving their tents, their horses and donkeys, and ran for their lives (7). The four lepers, who were among the most outcast and despised men of that time, were now used in the providence of God to announce the wonderful provisions that were evidences of the grace of God. For after the four men had eaten and drunk enough to satisfy their hunger, they carried off silver, gold, clothes and hid it for themselves (8).

Then it struck them all at once: "We're not doing right. This is a day of good news and we are keeping it to ourselves. If we wait until daylight, punishment will overtake us. Let's go at once and report this to the royal palace" (9). So they went and called out to the gatekeepers at Samaria and told them what they had found (10). The gatekeepers shouted the news, which eventually got to the palace. This awakened the king in the middle of the night (12). He was naturally skeptical at first, presuming this was a trick by the Arameans to lure them out of the city, so they could be captured (12c). Accordingly, some men were picked to take five horses that were left in Israel, and with two chariots, they were to go see if the report was true (13-15). They followed the trail of discarded clothes and belongings all the way down to the Jordan River, but they saw no Syrians/Arameans anywhere. So the messengers returned to report to the king the good news (15c).

With that, the gates of Samaria flew open and the starving people rushed out of the city trampling to death, in the pandemonium, the officer on whose arm the king leaned and who had scoffed at the prediction that food would be available. He never saw what he had so mockingly decried when Elisha had predicted what would take place that very next day.

God's Serious Warning to Those Who Disbelieve His Word - 7:16-20

Watch Making Light of God's Denunciations

Verses 16-17 recorded the fulfillment of the word of God that Elisha had spoken. It had come to pass exactly as God had spoken that word. Therefore, we cannot trifle with God's threatening's or escape his denunciations. While we would rather dwell on the mercies of God, nevertheless, God warns the ungodly about his punishments if there is no repentance in the interim.

If this officer of the king thought that God was too merciful to carry out his threats, apparently so did the people of Noah's day. Those of Sodom and Gomorrah thought the same thing. Verse 18 emphasizes that "It happened as the man of God had said to the king."

Watch for the Complete Fulfillment of the Warning

The king's officer, v. 19 repeated, had said God was going to have to open up windows in heaven if such a thing were going to happen – in other words it was just plain impossible. But the relief from the famine was so sudden, it was almost like windows had been flung open in the sky, for now there was plenty of food for all and it was very inexpensive at that!

Proverbs 13:13a says, "He who scorns instruction will pay for it." That king's officer certainly did, for he was trampled in the gate of Samaria as the rush was on to get food (20).

Conclusions

1. We must pay close attention to the sure and proven promises and threats from God, for they will certainly come to pass.

2. When God has spoken so clearly, why is it that mortals so frequently pay no attention to it, or think that God is so merciful that no judgment will come?

3. Can the same God who made the ax-head surface on the water also make miracles happen in our day?

4. Is our Lord one who can see everything that happens on earth and therefore we should be careful what we say or do?

Questions for Thought and Reflection

1. Is a miracle a violation of the natural law of God or is a miracle the introduction of some new law we had not known about, but God did?

2. Does God monitor the movements of all enemies around the world, or can these only be detected by ordinary acts of espionage and intelligence gathering?

3. Should we link any of our national disasters to our increased sin and wickedness in our culture?

4. How did God use panic of the enemy to bring relief to Israel? How can we pray for the same type of effects in our day when we are now involved in such badly divided times filled with such gross wickedness as a nation?

Lessons 13 & 14

Witnessing God's Providential Hand for Good and Bad

2 Kings 8:1 – 9:37; 13:14 - 25

Elisha The Prophet

The prophet Elisha had warned of an impending famine in the land. So, the woman from Shunem, who had shown an unbounded devotion and given loads of kindnesses to the prophet Elisha (2 Kings 4:8-36), appeared once again in our narrative. But this account seems to be out of chronological order, since Elisha does not appear in this account, only Elisha's old servant, Gehazi, who at the request of the king of Israel, Gehazi was recounting the events of the prophet's life to the king. The seven-year-famine mentioned here must have come somewhere in the middle of King Joram's reign, which famine must have been the one mentioned in 2 Kings 4:38.

If it is asked, "Then why was this account placed in this position in the text much later than when it seems to have occurred, the answer is that here was an example of an obedient woman and her son. They had heard the word of God and had acted in obedience to it. This was placed in juxtaposition to the two apparently unbelieving women, who had quarreled, because during the famine they became involved in a dispute that led to eating one of their sons but the other woman failed to keep her end of the bargain, but out of love hid her son so he would not be eaten! This other boy had been hidden and was being withheld from the woman whose son they had already eaten. Moreover, the triple affirmation of 7:16-20 that the relief of the famine had come, "Exactly as the man of God had said," is matched by 8:4-5, where the Shunammite's restored-to-life-son appeared at precisely that moment to confirm Gehazi's account of the special deeds done by Elisha. The word of God was altogether true, for all of this had been taking place out in the open before their very eyes!

Text: 2 Kings 8:1 – 9:37

Title or Subject of the Lesson: "Witnessing God's Providential Hand For Doing Good or Bad"

Focal Point: 8:19 "Nevertheless, for the sake of his servant David, the LORD was not willing to destroy Judah. He had promised to maintain a lamp for David and his descendants forever."

Homiletical Keyword: Instances

Interrogtive: What? (Are The Instances Where The Providential Hand Of God Could Be Seen Working Either For Or Against Israel And Yet Judah Was In The End Preserved?)

MEMORY VERSE: Same As Focal Point In 8:19.

The Outline

    I. In the King's Restoration of the Widow's Land – 8:1-6

   II. In God's Using a Pagan King to Discipline a Wicked Family – 8:7-15

 III. In God's Judging Wickedness in Judah – 8:16-29

 IV. In Anointing a New Kingly Line in Israel – 9:1-13

    V. In Fulfilling the Word of God for the Murder of an Innocent Man – 9:14- 37

 VI. In The Power of Elisha Even Though He Was Dead – 13:14-25

The Lesson

In The King's Restoration of a Widow's Land – 8:1-6

The Principle of Trusting a Word From God

The prophet Elisha had urged the woman from the town of Shunem, whose son he had restored to life to, "Go away with your family and stay for a while wherever you can, because the LORD has decreed a famine in the land that will last for seven years" (1b). This woman, who had been so faithful during the times when Elisha taught the word of God as part of his Bible study (2 Kings 4:23), yet once again was obedient to the word from God (2a). She and her family went into the land of the Philistines for seven years (2b). This time she did not try to counter what the prophet said, as she had when she was told by the prophet that she would have a son (4:16). By now she had learned to act on the basis of every word from God. Painful and difficult as it was, she relinquished working on her farm and being with her friends and possessions, for in obedience she moved away, just as did Abraham of old when he too was called by God to move from Ur. Verse 2 specifically noted that, "The woman proceeded to do as the man of God [had] said" (2a). Her obedience was immediate and complete.

Even though the famine had not arrived as yet, she must have left in the midst of general prosperity and plenty, yet there was not one word of skepticism or complaint on her part. Once she had heard the word of God, she acted on it right away! Here was the true nature of faith.

The Principle of Depending on the Providence of God

Previously, when Elisha had asked her if there was anything he could do for her when he and his servant were living in her home, she had primly replied that she did not need anything, nor did she need someone to speak on her behalf to the king or to the commander of the army (4:13), for she was among her own people and was satisfied. She may have had a trace of independence and self-sufficiency about her, in that she felt she had a hold on all that she needed. But in this world of changing circumstances and unknown vicissitudes, very few, if any, are beyond the reach of change and misfortune.

Apparently in her seven-year-absence from her land in Shunem, some encroaching neighbor, or perhaps even the royal crown itself, had seized the land as their own. Like Naomi, who had gone to Moab to avoid an earlier famine, she had gone away from her home full, but now the Lord had brought Naomi and this widow woman back empty (cf. Ruth 1:21). This is why we should not lay-up treasures on this earth, nor should we make our earthly inheritance our chief delight, for the inheritance we seek is one that is incorruptible and undefiled, one that does not fade away and is reserved in heaven for us.

It was at that very same moment that the servant of Elisha, Gehazi, happened to be in the royal court of the king. He was describing how Elisha had brought the son of this woman back to life, when all of a sudden this woman providentially arrived at the palace at the same time to beg the king to restore to her both her house and her land. Gehazi blurted out, "This is the [very] woman, my lord" (8:5). It looked like a chance meeting, but it had been arranged in the providence of God!

Believers should not call such instances "coincidences," for when we view the whole range of events in God's word and those in our own lives, as well as the range of events in history, we are forced to acknowledge that all of these events are evidences of the overruling hand of God, directing everything according to his infinite wisdom and his marvelous power. Some are willing to believe in the doctrine of *general providence*, but they wish to deny *particular providence* in such things as the fall of the sparrow, for instance. Every event, large or small, however, is either directed or allowed by our Heavenly Father's guiding hand. The fact that these prophecies of God were accomplished "just as the prophet or God had said" is enough to defeat the view that God is unconcerned about what might at first seem little, small, casual, or incidental events in the epic of life. Perhaps Pharaoh of Egypt looked on the exodus as a matter of chance or bad luck on his part, but Acts 4:27-28 says God had predicted Israel would stay in Egypt 430 years and then would come out of Egypt, "even on that self-same day!"

Thus, not only are the great outlines of our lives sketched by our Heavenly Father, but so are the small events and happenings that make up the larger ones, as well. To deny or reject the so-called "dot" (i.e., the precise event) in the will of God in his plan for our lives is to deny particular providence in favor of just a general providence of God. But he is Lord of both the general and particular providence at all times and in all places.

In God's Using a Pagan King to Discipline a Wicked Family -8:7-15

God's Work in the Lives of Those Who are Sick

Some of the favored times for God to speak to his men and women, whether they are believers or not, is when they are sick and on a bed of pain. It is at least to the pagan king's credit that he sent by the hand of his associate for Elisha the prophet, whom he had heard was visiting Damascus, to see if he would get well (7-8). This was a lot better than King Ahaziah, the Israelite king (!), who sent messengers off to inquire of Beelzebub, the Philistine god of Ekron, in order to learn if he would get well or not (2 Kings 1:2-6). What a contrast! Ben-Hadad, the king in Aram, must have recalled how Naaman received healing from the prophet Elijah. Note that Gehazi is not mentioned in this text, so this event must have come later, since by now he had been dismissed from helping Elisha.

The reason that Elisha was in Damascus may have been to fulfill the command that Elijah had given some time ago to anoint the next king of Syria (1 Kings 19:15). But interestingly enough,

King Ben Hadad asked for no cure; he only wanted to know if he would get well. Was this an indication of his lack of faith? But by now he knew that ADONAI alone held the knowledge of the future and the power to affect the present as well. Such ambitions would preempt King Ben-Hadad's recovery from his illness. Thus, Hazael was told that the reigning king would die, not from his sickness, but his demise would come from Hazael's secret desire to usurp his master's role as king. Therefore, Elisha's answer seemed to be deliberately ambiguous, but it was clear in its fulfillment that he was 100% accurate as God's word always is.

God's Work in Connection with Human Freedom

It was not a normal procedure for God to inform people of his forthcoming works, for "Known only to God are all his works from the beginning of the world" (Acts 15:18). But there is a freedom given in part to mortals because we stand under the government of the Lord himself, who maintains order. For even the case where Hazael was told that he would be king, it still was within his several options to refuse to stoop to such a low level to establish his kingship by his own hands. If Hazael trusted Elisha's words, then he should have rested secure in that fact and not to have forced the issue, for no one is justified in doing sin, not even to make a prediction of God come true! God can fulfill his own word without our help!

Hazael could not plead that possible providential opportunities were proof that God approved of the course of action he took in smothering the sick king to death in order to gain the throne. Hazael pretended to be shocked by the disclosure of such predicted atrocities that he was about to commit (13), but his humility and self-deprecating words were hypocritical. Did he not know that in his own character *he* was fully capable of carrying out this event? Neither Elisha nor God were knowing, or even unknowing, accomplices to Hazael's treacherous acts; he was responsible for all that he had become and now was.

In God's Judging Wickedness in Judah – 8:16-29

Saved by a Divine Promise

It has been 17 years since the patrimony of Naboth's vineyard had been wrestled away from him and a false claim of blasphemy was used as the basis for his death (1 Kings 21). Now, once again, all the actors of the original cast and scenery of that act were present. The account could easily be said to have begun in Ramoth-Gilead, where King Joram of Israel was continuing to walk in all the evil ways of the kings of Israel.

However, there is another son, with a name identical to name of a northern king of Israel, King Jehoram, who arrives as king in Jerusalem of Judah, as the son of King Jehoshaphat at 32 years of age. This son, however, was married to Ahab and Jezebel's daughter Athaliah. It now appeared that the southern two tribes were going to go off the rails of righteousness the way of the ten northern tribes of Israel had gone, for this King Jehoram also did evil in the eyes of the Lord.

However, despite all these failures, God had given his word to David that he would preserve a "lamp" in all Israel for David and his descendants forever (19). Here was the major difference between the two kingdoms in Israel. God would preserve the line of David in southern Judah, because of his own oath to maintain his promise to David. Meanwhile, the kingdom of Edom rebelled against Judah and Jehoram almost lost his life as he broke through the surrounding Edomite chariots and army of Edom narrowly to escape being captured or be killed (21). Moreover, the city that was close to the Philistines, Libnah, revolted at the same time and broke away from Judah's control. It appeared that the kingdom of Judah was systematically being reduced and weakened, as her sin mounted up against her and before God, just as it had happened to northern Israel.

Another Judean King Compromises

Jehoram's son, Ahaziah, succeeded his father as king in Judah when he was 22 years old (25), but with a pagan mother like Athaliah and a maternal grandfather like Omri, what could one expect? (26). He favored going the way of the house of Ahab up north, rather than following David as his model. In fact, he too joined Joram son of Ahab to fight Hazael king of Syria (27-28).

King Joram was wounded in his battle with King Hazael, so he returned to Jezreel to recover (28b). But Omri's dynasty (in the line of King Ahab) from the northern tribes of Israel was now setting the tone for both north and south and it was not pleasing to the Lord.

In Anointing a New Kingly Line in Israel – 9:1-13

The Prophet Elisha, Under God, Directs History

Elisha designated one of the sons of the prophets to take a flask of oil and run as fast as he could to Ramoth-Gilead, where he was to anoint an army captain named Jehu, son of Jehoshaphat, son of Nimshi (9:1-2a). When he got to Ramoth-Gilead, he was to get Jehu away from his companions and pour the oil of inauguration on his head as he said, "This is what the LORD, the God of Israel says: 'I anoint you king over the LORD's people Israel. You are to destroy the house of Ahab, your master, and I will avenge the blood of my servants the prophets and the blood of all the LORD's servant shed by Jezebel'" (6-7). Jehu was to cut off from Ahab every male, slave or free, and to make Ahab's house like the now-destroyed house of Jeroboam I, son of Nebat, and like the house of Baasha son of Ahijah (8b-9). Worse still, Jehu was to deal with Jezebel, for dogs would devour her on the very plot of ground she stole from Naboth the Jezreelite (10).

The Army Commanders Suddenly Realize Jehu is the New King of Israel

When the messenger from the school of the prophets had finished the task that Elisha sent him on, as instructed, he opened the door of the house he had used for the brief anointing ceremony of Jehu and fled as fast as he had come (10b). As the army commander, Jehu emerged from the house, after this son of the prophets had suddenly left. The officers Jehu had been sitting with on the steps to the house wanted to know what he had said. "Was everything all right," they inquired. Even more disparagingly, they asked, "What did this madman/crazy-fellow come to you for?" (11b). That is what they thought about God's prophets and their messages: they were all crazy people, just out of their minds!

Jehu tried to put the questions off by saying, "You know the man and the sort of things he says" (11c). But his officer-buddies would not be put off. "Come on," they coaxed, "Tell us." (12a). Jehu then told them he had just been anointed king of Israel by the word of the Lord. With that, they spread their cloaks under him on the steps they had been sitting on and blew a *shofar* (ram's horn) yelling, "Jehu is king" (13). A palace change in the government had just happened!

In Fulfilling the Word of God for the Murders of Innocent Men – 9:14-37

The King of Israel and The King of Judah are Killed

No sooner had Jehu been anointed as king than off he rode like a "madman" (20c) to carry out his mission of killing King Joram of Israel. Joram had been convalescing at the summer palace of Jezreel from the wounds he had received from a previous battle at Ramoth-Gilead (15). However, as Jehu approached Jezreel (16), the watchmen on the Jezreel tower reported that he saw some troops approaching (17). Joram ordered him to have a horseman go meet this party and find out what their purpose was in riding towards them (17b-18a). Jehu answered the messenger roughly and told him to fall in behind him. When this was reported by the lookout on the tower of Jezreel, a second horseman was sent out, with the same results. Moreover, the lookout reported that the driving was so furious it could have been none other than the reckless riding of Jehu, who was King Joram's commander at Ramoth-Gilead (20b).

When this second rider did not return either, Joram ordered that his chariot be hitched up and that he, and Ahaziah, king of Judah, who was visiting the wounded northern king, should ride out together to confront Jehu and his retinue (21) to see what was the matter.

When Joram met Jehu, he asked Jehu, "Have you come in peace?" (22). But Jehu retorted, "How can there be peace, as long as all the idolatry and witchcraft of your mother Jezebel abounds?" (22). Then Joram realized that Jehu was up to no good; so, he turned his steed and chariot around, calling out to King Ahaziah of Judah, "Treachery, Ahaziah" (23). With that Jehu drew his bow and shot Joram between the shoulders so that the arrow pierced through to his heart and he died (24).

Jehu ordered Bidkar, his chariot officer, to pick up Joram's corpse and throw him into the field that had belonged to Naboth the Jezreelite, the very man he had dispossessed and murdered (25). Jehu recalled when he and Bidkar were riding behind King Ahab, that the LORD had made a prophecy against this king for the unjust way Ahab and Jezebel had treated Naboth by stealing his vineyard (25b). This prophecy he heard was this: "Yesterday I saw the blood of Naboth and the blood of his sons, declares the LORD, and I will surely make you pay for it on this plot of ground, declares the LORD" (26). Therefore, this is what they did with Joram "in accordance with the word of the LORD" (26d, cf. 1 Kings 21:29c) – they dumped his body on the field of Naboth's vineyard to rot.

Ahaziah was then chased up the road to Beth-Haggan by Jehu and he too was wounded near Ibleam, but he escaped to Megiddo, where later he too died (27). Then Ahaziah's servants took Ahaziah back to Jerusalem where he was buried in the City of David (28).

Queen Jezebel is Killed

Meanwhile Jezebel was fixing herself up with all her cosmetics, apparently to make herself presentable in order to vamp the new conqueror Jehu (30). Jezebel must have realized that a rebellion was under way, for when Jehu rode up to the summer palace at Jezreel, she called out, "Have your come in peace, Zimri, you murderer of your master?" (31). Zimri was an earlier insurrectionist in Israel's history, who had destroyed the family of King Baasha (1 Kings 16:12-13), so the word must have gotten out that Jezebel's son Joram was now dead. Was she trying to seduce Jehu with her appearance and willful arts of femininity, hoping thereby to save her neck from the same ending?

Whatever she was trying to do, Jehu was having none of it, for he was all business. He called out, "Who is on my side?" With that, two or three palace eunuchs looked out a window of an upper story at him (32). "Throw her down!" Jehu ordered, and that is what these men did (33a). Her blood spattered against the wall as the horses of the Jehu's retinue parked in front of the palace trampled her underfoot (33b). Jehu had nonchalantly gone into the palace and eaten and drunk without giving it all a second thought, but then he remembered Jezebel probably lay dead outside, so he gave the order to bury her, for after all she was queen of the land. However, when the servants went to bury her, the dogs had so devoured her that there was nothing left except her skull, her feet and her hands (35).

This all happened in accordance with the word of the Lord that Elijah had spoken in 1 Kings 21:23, which had predicted, dogs will devour Jezebel's flesh on the very plot of ground she and her husband had taken from the vineyard belonging to Naboth (36-37). That, of course, is exactly what happened.

In the Conclusion to Elisha's Life – 13:14-25

The Summary of the Lives and Ministries of the Prophets Elijah and Elisha

Elijah and Elisha had led the renewal movement in the ten northern tribes of Israel from 875 B.C.E. – 848 (in the case of Elijah) and from 848 - 797 B.C.E. (in the case of Elisha). It had lasted for over three quarters of a century. These years came to a climax in the destructive zeal of King Jehu, who annihilated the house of Omri and Ahab, and it also brought a temporary halt to the house of Judah as well, since the king of Judah had married the daughter of Ahab and Jezebel.

The books of 1 and 2 Kings, with their 47 chapters, record the devastating history of Israel, yet about a third of these chapters in 1 and 2 Kings (1 Kings 17-22, 2 Kings 1-9, 13), actually 15 chapters in all, were devoted to the ministries of Elijah and Elisha, who called for a renewal and revival, especially in the ten northern tribes of Israel. Seldom have two more impressive agents of God appeared, precisely at the divinely ordained moment, to call a wayward nation back to God in repentance and revival.

2 Kings 13 provides us with our last glimpse of Elisha, even though his activity and name has become quiescent in 2 Kings' chapters of 10, 11 and 12. Once again the narrative was shaped apart from a strict chronological order to the text, for in 2 Kings 13:10-13, where the reign, death and burial of King Jehoash is given, yet oddly enough in 2 Kings 13:14, after this king has been buried in the previous verse, he visits Elisha! So once again the text is not necessarily in chronological order.

Jehoash visited the prophet Elisha, for the prophet was on his death bed at the time (13:14a). The king wept for the prophet, as he honored him by calling him, "My father, my father!" (14b). He furthermore attributed to Elisha the same words Elisha had cried out when Elijah had been transported to heaven in front of his eyes by a whirlwind, for he now said about the prophet Elisha, "the chariots and horsemen of Israel" (14c). In saying this, King Jehoash acknowledged that Elisha was the true source of the nation of Israel's defense and national security. This prophet was more valuable than all the military armaments of Israel put together. Men and women like this are just as valuable in our day and age as well, for they are to be preferred over all the sophisticated weaponry and hardware any nation could muster for its defense.

Elisha, now on his death bed, urges the king to get a bow and some arrows and open the east window (15a). Then Elisha put his hands on the king's hands as he ordered him to shoot the arrow from the bow. As the king did so, Elisha cried out, "The LORD's arrow of victory over Aram!" (17a). Then, the prophet predicted, the king would destroy the Arameans at Aphek (17b-c).

Elisha also ordered that the king take the arrows and strike them on the ground, but the king only struck the ground with them three times (18). This angered Elisha, for he had hoped the king would strike the ground five or six times, for then he, as Elisha explained, would have completely destroyed Aram/Syria, but as it was, Jehoash's victories over Aram/Syria would be limited to three conquests (19).

Elisha died and was buried, but that was not the end of his story (20). For Moabite raiders invaded the country of Israel as they did every Spring. Once, then, when an Israelite funeral procession was in progress, the Israelites were on their way to bury a man, when all of a sudden they saw the dreaded Moabite raiders coming in their direction. In their haste, they threw the corpse of the deceased man on what turned out to be Elisha's tomb, and rushed off to avoid capture. But when the dead man's body touched Elisha's bones, he suddenly came to life again and he stood on his feet (21). I wonder what they said when he may have passed them as both the burial party and the corpse raced back to town in a dead heat!

Our narrative of these two prophets ends with Hazael of Syria oppressing Israel (22), yet the Lord was gracious to Israel, because of his covenant with Abraham, Isaac, and Jacob. Our Lord was unwilling to destroy Israel or banish them from his presence forever, since he had given his word in his promise-plan to the Patriarchs and to King David. His promise would not fail!

Conclusions

1. The Covenant God made with the Patriarchs and David is irrevocable (Rom 11:20). It will stand firm to the end.
2. The power of God can be seen even in death as God has the power to raise from the dead a man who merely touched the bones of his prophet Elisha. What must the power of this prophet have been in his lifetime, if this was the residual effect of his work with God after he had died?
3. Let us acknowledge the hand of God in both general and particular providence over men, families, congregations and nations.
4. God does hold mortals responsible for the choices we make, for even they are part of God's ultimate design and plans.

Questions for Thought or Discussion

1. Does the providence of God cover just the large areas of our lives but not the specifics of life, such as where I should go to school, to whom should I get married, or where will I spend my life working?
2. Do the evil effects of a bad family line pass down to the children? Always? What can be done to avoid such transmission?
3. Why would God choose an army captain to carry out his work? Does this mean that God directed all the evil he did or did God merely permit it?
4. What do you think about a dead man being brought back to life after merely touching the bones of Elisha? What does the Tanakh say about life after death?

Elijah and Elisha
in Jewish Tradition

We are fortunate to have in our possession a large collection of materials in rabbinical literature on the prophet Elijah which help broaden our understanding of this man. This prophet has so captured the thoughts and imagination of the Jewish community that there are loads of stories about him, both from the ancient and Medieval rabbis. Add to this, Elijah appears frequently in Muslim traditions as well. Most significant among all these numerous tales recounting Elijah's exploits and miraculous deeds was his supernatural removal from this earth.

The rabbinical literature on Elijah consists of two types: *halachah,* meaning the "rule," consisting of legal materials on the law of God, and *aggadah* meaning the "narration," i.e., the sermonic material. No claim was made for the truthfulness of these legends, maxims, or parables, but they were offered as a way of helping Jewish people gain some understanding of the spiritual achievements of Elijah. In fact, the *aggadic* materials on Elijah far outweigh the references to any other Biblical character.

One such story has the prophet Elijah comforting Messiah as he awaits his time to come back to earth again! This is not to claim that Jewish thought taught that Yeshua was the Messiah. As a matter of fact, Jewish tradition taught that there will actually be two future Messiahs: Messiah ben Yoseph, who will suffer and die in the Gog-Magog encounter in the last days, and Messiah ben David, the one who will conquer the armies of wickedness and reign supreme in the time of the Kingdom. However, between the coming of the two Messiahs, there will be a period of forty-five days, during which time Elijah will read aloud from the Book of Jasher (cf. Jos 10:13; 2 Sam 1:18-27). It is said that this reading will have the powerful effect on making the Earth itself swallow up the enemies of Israel!

Elijah is especially prominent in Jewish thought and ritual in what is known in the Jewish tradition as the *havdalah*, which marks the end of the Sabbath. At that time, songs are sung about Elijah. One particular line in one of those songs is: *The prophet Elijah, the Tishbite from Gilead, may he come to us soon with the son of David, the Messiah.*

The other significant reference to Elijah can be found in the Passover Seder. A special cup and an empty place were specially reserved for him at the table. Then, at a designated moment in the Seder, one of the children opens the door to see if the prophet Elijah is coming to join the family celebrating Passover this night.

Both Elijah and Elisha were used by God to call an apostate nation of Israel and Judah back to the Lord. Yet, even after the death of both of these men, Malachi 4:5-6 announces that Elijah the prophet will yet come once more and in that coming he will avert the curse God had placed over Israel. John the Immerser began that work in his day, but it still remains to be completed. In that final day, according to Revelation 11:3-13, our Lord will send Elijah and Moses for three and a half years during the time of Jacob's trouble (Jer. 30:7), also known as the "great tribulation" (Matt. 24:21; Rev. 7:14).

Both Elijah and Elisha were critical in the great period of the prophets in the *Tenach*. Even though their ministry was powerful both in word and deed, it still is not finished yet, but will be soon, for Elijah must come before Messiah returns a second time.

Select Bibliography

Bronner, Leah. *The Stories of Elijah and Elisha*. Leiden: E. J. Brill, 1968.

Davis, Dale Ralph. *The Wisdom and the Folly: An Exposition of the Book of I Kings*. Ross-shire, Scotland: Christian Focus, 2002.

_____. *The Power and the Fury*. Ross-shire, Scotland: Christian Focus, 2005.

Herschel, Abraham J. *The Prophets, 2 vols*. New York: Harper and Row, 1955.

Hubbard, Robert L. Jr. *First and Second Kings*. Chicago: Moody Press, 1991.

Keller, W. Phillip. *Elijah: Prophet of Power*. Waco: Word Books, 1980.

Krummacher, F. W. *Elisha: A Prophet for Our Times*. Grand Rapids: Baker Book House, 1976.

_____. *The Last Days of Elisha*. Grand Rapids: Baker Book House, 1981.

Leithart, Peter. *1 & 2 Kings*. Grand Rapids: Brazos Press, 2006.

Meyer, F. B. *Elijah and the Secret of His Power*. Fort Washington, PA: Christian Literature Crusade, 1972.

Pink, A. W. *The Life of Elijah*. London: The Banner of Truth Trust, 1963.

Varner, Will. *The Chariot of Israel: Exploits of the Prophet Elijah*. Bellmawr, NJ: The Friends of Israel, 1984.

First Time in History!

General Editor: Rabbi Barry Rubin
Theological Editor: Dr. John Fischer

The Complete Jewish Study Bible

Insights for Jews and Christians
—Dr. David H. Stern

A One-of-a-Kind Study Bible that illuminates the Jewish background and context of God's word so it is more fully understandable. Uses the updated *Complete Jewish Bible* text by David H. Stern, including notes from the *Jewish New Testament Commentary* and contributions from Scholars listed below. 1990 pages.

< Hardcover Edition

Hardback	978-1619708679	$49.95
Flexisoft	978-1619708693	$79.95
Leather	978-1619708709	$139.95

Leather Edition w/color gift box   Flexisoft Edition w/color sleeve

CONTRIBUTORS & SCHOLARS

Rabbi Dr. Glenn Blank	Forbes	Rabbi Barney Kasdan	Rosenberg
Dr. Michael Brown	Rabbi Dr. David	Dr. Craig S. Keener	Rabbi Isaac Roussel
Rabbi Steven Bernstein	Friedman	Rabbi Elliot Klayman	Dr. Michael Rydelnik
Rabbi Joshua	Dr. Arnold	Jordan Gayle Levy	Dr. Jeffrey Seif
Brumbach	Fruchtenbaum	Dr. Ronald Moseley	Rabbi Tzahi Shapira
Rabbi Ron Corbett	Dr. John Garr	Rabbi Dr. Rich Nichol	Dr. David H. Stern
Pastor Ralph Finley	Pastor David Harris	Rabbi Mark J. Rantz	Dr. Bruce Stokes
Rabbi Dr. John Fischer	Benjamin Juster	Rabbi Russ Resnik	Dr. Tom Tribelhorn
Dr. Patrice Fischer	Rabbi Dr. Daniel Juster	Dr. Richard Robinson	Dr. Forrest Weiland
Rebbitzen Malkah	Dr. Walter C. Kaiser	Rabbi Dr. Jacob	Dr. Marvin Wilson

QUOTES BY JEWISH SCHOLARS & SAGES

Dr. Daniel Boyarin
Dr. Amy-Jill Levine
Rabbi Jonathan Sacks
Rabbi Gamaliel
Rabbi Hillel
Rabbi Shammai
Rabbi Akiva
Maimonides
and many more

Complete Jewish Bible: *An English Version*

—Dr. David H. Stern (Available March 2017)

Now, the most widely used Messianic Jewish Bible around the world, has updated text with introductions added to each book, written from a biblically Jewish perspective. The CJB is a unified Jewish book, a version for Jews and non-Jews alike; to connect Jews with the Jewishness of the Messiah, and non-Jews with their Jewish roots. Names and terms are returned to their original Hebrew and presented in easy-to-understand transliterations, enabling the reader to say them the way *Yeshua* (Jesus) did! 1728 pages.

Paperback	978-1936716845	$29.95
Hardcover	978-1936716852	$34.95
Flexisoft Cover	978-1936716869	$49.95

Jewish New Testament
—Dr. David H. Stern

The New Testament is a Jewish book, written by Jews, initially for Jews. Its central figure was a Jew. His followers were all Jews; yet no other version really communicates its original, essential Jewishness. Uses neutral terms and Hebrew names. Highlights Jewish references and corrects mistranslations. Freshly translated into English from Greek, this is a must read to learn about first-century faith. 436 pages

Hardback	978-9653590069	**JB02**	$19.99
Paperback	978-9653590038	**JB01**	$14.99
Spanish	978-1936716272	**JB17**	$24.99

Also available in French, German, Polish, Portuguese and Russian.

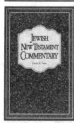

Jewish New Testament Commentary
—Dr. David H. Stern

This companion to the *Jewish New Testament* enhances Bible study. Passages and expressions are explained in their original cultural context. 15 years of research. 960 pages.

Hardback	978-9653590083	**JB06**	$34.99
Paperback	978-9653590113	**JB10**	$29.99

Is Christ *Really* The "End of The Law"?
Another Look at *Telos* in Romans 10:4
—Drs. Jeffrey and Barri Cae Seif

"There are few Pauline statements more controversial than Romans 10:4, specifically the meaning of the word τέλος, telos.

τέλος γὰρ νόμου Χριστὸς εἰς δικαιοσύνην παντὶ τῷ πιστεύοντι.

The verse has traditionally been rendered, "For Christ is the *end* of the Law for righteousness to everyone who believes." Some say, "For the *goal* at which the Torah aims is the Messiah" while others prefer *new beginning*. Still others offer, "For Messiah is the *end* of the Torah, that everyone who has faith may be justified" or "Messiah is the *culmination* of the Torah so that there may be righteousness for everyone believes." 179 Pages

Paperback	978-1733935418	$21.99

Messianic Jewish Orthodoxy
The Essence of Our Faith, History and Best Practices
–Dr. Jeffrey Seif, General Editor

A work from the moderate, conservative center of the Messianic Jewish revival. This book speaks to the interests that group and the Church have in Jews, Israel and eschatology, with a need for a more-balanced consideration of faith, theology and practice—from Jewish perspectives.

This is vital for the many tens of thousands of Jews who have come to faith and who participate in Messianic Jewish experience and also those who frequent churches. Our non-Jewish friends who associate with the Messianic Jewish movement will find this book beneficial as well. It represents some of our best thinking and practice. 314 pages

Paperback	978-1733935425	$26.99

The Lives and Ministries of ELIJAH and ELISHA
Demonstrating the Wonderful Power of the Word of God
—Dr. Walter C. Kaiser, Jr.

It's no wonder Old Testament professor Walt Kaiser is one of America's most beloved Bible expositors. This series of studies on Elijah and Elisha is vintage Kaiser, interspersed with his trademark humor. Organized in outline format, it offers an easy-to-follow look at the lives of two of the most famous and lively prophets ever to grace the pages of the Old Testament. Highly recommended to enhance anyone's study of the Scriptures! 182 pages

Paperback	978-1733935449	$17.99

Social Justice The Bible and Application for Our Times
—Daniel C. Juster

In this work, addressing many of the social justice issues of today, one of the more seasoned Messianic Jewish leaders and scholars, Dr. Dan Juster, offers his thoughts. Not an academic book, we read what this well-known pioneer of Messianic Judaism, director of Tikkun International, founding president of the Union of Messianic Jewish Congregations and senior pastor of Beth Messiah Congregation from 1978-2012, thinks about the way our world is today. You will find his thoughts challenging and surprising. 122 pages

Paperback	978-1733935456	$12.99

The Book of Ruth
This delightful version of *The Book of Ruth* includes the full text from the *Complete Jewish Bible* on the left page of the two-page spread. On the right are artful illustrations with brief story summaries that can be read to young children. Can be read any time during the year, but especially on *Shavuot* (Pentecost), the anniversary of the giving of the Torah on Mount Sinai and when the Holy Spirit was poured out on Yeshua's disciples (Acts 2). *The Book of Ruth* points to Yeshua as the ultimate Kinsman Redeemer.
6 x 9 inches, 26 pages with full color illustrations.

Paperback	978-1-936716-94-4	$ 9.99

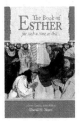

The Book of Esther
This delightful version of *The Book of Esther* includes the full text from the *Complete Jewish Bible* on the left page of the two-page spread. On the right are artful illustrations with brief story summaries that can be read to young children. Can be read any time during the year, but especially during *Purim*, the festival that celebrates how Queen Esther risked her life and became a vessel for the deliverance of her people Israel. Though God is not mentioned, Mordecai and Esther humbled themselves before God by fasting and praying, which showed dependence upon him. God answered and delivered his people while bringing the proud Haman to justice.
6 x 9 inches, 34 pages with full color illustrations.

Paperback	978-1-936716-95-1	$ 9.99

Dear You
Letters of Identity in Yeshua ~ for Women ~
—Victoria Humphrey

Dear You is about discovering the truth of who you are as a beloved and courageous daughter of the King. It is an invitation to uncover what Elohim says about you through Scripture, silencing all other noise that vies to define you. While weaving together personal testimonies from other women, along with an opportunity to unearth your own unique story, it presents the challenge to leave a shallow life behind by taking a leap into the abundant life Yeshua offers. 232 Pages

Paperback	978-1-7339354-0-1	$19.99

A Life of Favor
A Family Therapist Examines the Story of Joseph and His Brothers
—Rabbi Russell Resnik, MA, LPCC

Favor is an inherent part of God's reality as Father, and properly understood, is a source of blessing to those who want to know him. The story of Jacob's sons points to a life of favor that can make a difference in our lives today. Excellent insight—judgments in exegesis are matched by skillful use of counseling principles and creative applications to contemporary situations in life and in the family. —Walter C. Kaiser, Jr. President Emeritus, Gordon-Conwell Theological Seminary, Hamilton, Mass. 212 Pages

Paperback	978-1936716913	$19.99

Will the Nazi Eagle Rise Again?
What the Church Needs to Know about BDS and Other Forces of Anti-Semitism
–David Friedman, Ph.D.

This is the right book at the right time. exposing the roots of Anti-Semitism being resurrected in our days, especially in our Christian Church.
—Dr. Hans-Jörg Kagi, Teacher, Theologian, Basle, Switzerland
Timely and important response to the dangerous hatred of the State of Israel that is growing in society and in the Church. 256 pages

Paperback	978-1936716876	$19.99

The Day Jesus Did Tikkun Olam
—Richard A. Robinson, Ph.D.

Easy-to-read, yet scholarly, explores ancient Jewish and Christian scriptures, relevant stories and biblical parallels, to explain the most significant Jewish value—*tikkun olam*—making this world a better place. This is a tenet of both religions, central to the person of Jesus himself. 146 pages
—Murray Tilles, Director, Light of Messiah Ministries; M.Div.
A wealth of scholarship and contemporary relevance with great insight into Jewish ethics and the teachings of Jesus.
—Dr. Richard Harvey, Senior Researcher, Jews for Jesus

Paperback	978-1-936716-98-2	$ 18.99

Jewish Giftedness & World Redemption
The Calling of Israel
—Jim Melnick

All things are mortal but the Jew; all other forces pass, but he remains. What is the secret of his immortality?

—Mark Twain, Concerning the Jews, *Harper's Magazine*, September, 1899.

The most comprehensive research of the unique achievements of the Jewish people. The author comes up with the only reason that makes sense of this mystery.

—Daniel C. Juster, Th.D., Restoration from Zion of Tikkun International

Paperback (280 Pages)   978-1-936716-88-3 $24.99

Messianic Judaism *A Modern Movement With an Ancient Past*
—David H. Stern

An updated discussion of the history, ideology, theology and program for Messianic Judaism. A challenge to both Jews and non-Jews who honor Yeshua to catch the vision of Messianic Judaism. 312 pages

Paperback   978-1880226339   **LB62** $17.99

Restoring the Jewishness of the Gospel
A Message for Christians
—David H. Stern

Introduces Christians to the Jewish roots of their faith, challenges some conventional ideas, and raises some neglected questions: How are both the Jews and "the Church" God's people? Is the Law of Moses in force today? Filled with insight! Endorsed by Dr. Darrell L. Bock. 110 pages

English - Paperback   978-1880226667   **LB70** $9.99
Spanish - Paperback   978-9653590175   **JB14** $9.99

The Return of the Kosher Pig *The Divine Messiah in Jewish Thought*
—Rabbi Tzahi Shapira

The subject of Messiah fills many pages of rabbinic writings. Hidden in those pages is a little known concept that the Messiah has the same authority given to God. Based on the Scriptures and traditional rabbinic writings, this book shows the deity of Yeshua from a new perspective. You will see that the rabbis of old expected the Messiah to be divine. Softcover, 352 pages.

"One of the most interesting and learned tomes I have ever read. Contained within its pages is much with which I agree, some with which I disagree, and much about which I never thought. Rabbi Shapria's remarkable book cannot be ignored."

—Dr. Paige Patterson, President, Southwest Baptist Theological Seminary

Paperback   978-1936716456   **LB81** $ 39.99

Messianic Jewish Commentary Series

Matthew Presents Yeshua, King Messiah
—Rabbi Barney Kasdan

Few commentators are able to truly present Yeshua in his Jewish context of his background, his family, even his religion. This commentator is well versed with first-century Jewish practices and thought, as well as the historical and cultural setting of the day, and the 'traditions of the Elders' that Yeshua so often spoke about. 448 pages

| Paperback | 978-1936716265 | **LB76** | $29.99 |

Rabbi Paul Enlightens the Ephesians on Walking with Messiah Yeshua
—Rabbi Barney Kasdan

The Ephesian were a diverse group of Jews and Gentiles, united together in Messiah. They definitely had an impact on the first century world in which they lived. But the Rabbi was not just writing to that local group. What is Paul saying to us? 160 pages.

| Paperback | 978-11936716821 | **LB99** | $17.99 |

Paul Presents to the Philippians Unity in the Messianic Community
—R. Sean Emslie

A worthy read and an appropriate study for any Messianic Jewish *talmid* or Christian disciple of Yeshua wanting to fairly and faithfully examine apostolic teaching. Emslie's investigation offers a keenly diligent analysis and faithfully responsible apostolic viewpoint. 165 pages

| Paperback | 978-1733935432 - Coming by June 30, 2020 | $18.99 |

James the Just Presents Application of Torah
—Dr. David Friedman

James (Jacob) one of the Epistles written to first century Jewish followers of Yeshua. Dr. David Friedman, a former Professor of the Israel Bible Institute has shed new light for Christians from this very important letter. 133 pages

| Paperback | 978-1936716449 | **LB82** | $14.99 |

John's Three Letters on Hope, Love and Covenant Fidelity
—Rabbi Joshua Brumbach

The Letters of John include some of the most beloved and often-quoted portions of scripture. Most people – scholars included – are confident they already have John's letters figured out. But do they really? There is a need for a fresh, post-supersessionist reading of John's letters that challenges common presuppositions regarding their purpose, message and relevance. 168 pages

| Paperback | 978-1-7339354-6-3 Coming by June 30, 2020 | $19.99 |

Jude On Faith and the Destructive Influence of Heresy
—Rabbi Joshua Brumbach

Almost no other canonical book has been as neglected and overlooked as the Epistle of Jude. This little book may be small, but it has a big message that is even more relevant today as when it was originally written. 100 pages

| Paperback | 978-1-936716-78-4 | **LB97** | $14.99 |

Yochanan (John) Presents the Revelation of Yeshua the Messiah
—Rabbi Gavriel Lumbroso

The Book of Revelation is perhaps the most mysterious, difficult-to-understand book in all of the Bible. Scholar after scholar, theologian after theologian have wrestled with all the strange visions, images and messages given by Yochanan (John), one of Yeshua's apostles. 206 pages

| Paperback | 978-1-936716-93-7 | $19.99 |

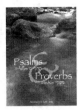

Psalms & Proverbs *Tehillim* תְּהִלִּים-*Mishlei* מִשְׁלֵי
—Translated by Dr. David Stern

Contemplate the power in these words anytime, anywhere: Psalms-*Tehillim* offers uplifting words of praise and gratitude, keeping us focused with the right attitude; Proverbs-*Mishlei* gives us the wisdom for daily living, renewing our minds by leading us to examine our actions, to discern good from evil, and to decide freely to do the good. Makes a wonderful and meaningful gift. 224 pages.

Paperback	978-1936716692	**LB90**	$9.99

At the Feet of Rabbi Gamaliel
Rabbinic Influence in Paul's Teachings
—David Friedman, Ph.D.

Paul (Shaul) was on the "fast track" to becoming a sage and Sanhedrin judge, describing himself as passionate for the Torah and the traditions of the fathers, typical for an aspiring Pharisee: "…trained at the feet of Gamaliel in every detail of the Torah of our forefathers. I was a zealot for God, as all of you are today" (Acts 22.3, CJB). Did Shaul's teachings reflect Rabbi Gamaliel's instructions? Did Paul continue to value the Torah and Pharisaic tradition? Did Paul create a 'New' Theology? The results of the research within these pages and its conclusion may surprise you. 100 pages.

Paperback	978-1936716753	**LB95**	$8.99

Debranding God *Revealing His True Essence*
—Eduardo Stein

The process of 'debranding' God is to remove all the labels and fads that prompt us to understand him as a supplier and ourselves as the most demanding of customers. Changing our perception of God also changes our perception of ourselves. In knowing who we are in relationship to God, we discover his, and our, true essence. 252 pages.

Paperback	978-1936716708	**LB91**	$16.99

Under the Fig Tree *Messianic Thought Through the Hebrew Calendar*
—Patrick Gabriel Lumbroso

Take a daily devotional journey into the Word of God through the Hebrew Calendar and the Biblical Feasts. Learn deeper meaning of the Scriptures through Hebraic thought. Beautifully written and a source for inspiration to draw closer to Adonai every day. 407 pages.

Paperback	978-1936716760	**LB96**	$25.99

Under the Vine *Messianic Thought Through the Hebrew Calendar*
—Patrick Gabriel Lumbroso

Journey daily through the Hebrew Calendar and Biblical Feasts into the B'rit Hadashah (New Testament) Scriptures as they are put in their rightful context, bringing Judaism alive in it's full beauty. Messianic faith was the motor and what gave substance to Abraham's new beliefs, hope to Job, trust to Isaac, vision to Jacob, resilience to Joseph, courage to David, wisdom to Solomon, knowledge to Daniel, and divine Messianic authority to Yeshua. 412 pages.

Paperback	978-1936716654	**LB87**	$25.99

Come and Worship *Ways to Worship from the Hebrew Scriptures*
—Compiled by Barbara D. Malda

We were created to worship. God has graciously given us many ways to express our praise to him. Each way fits a different situation or moment in life, yet all are intended to bring honor and glory to him. When we believe that he is who he says he is [see *His Names are Wonderful!*] and that his Word is true, worship flows naturally from our hearts to his. 128 pages.

Paperback	978-1936716678	**LB88**	$9.99

His Names Are Wonderful
Getting to Know God Through His Hebrew Names
—Elizabeth L. Vander Meulen and Barbara D. Malda

In Hebrew thought, names did more than identify people; they revealed their nature. God's identity is expressed not in one name, but in many. This book will help readers know God better as they uncover the truths in his Hebrew names. 160 pages.

Paperback	978-1880226308	**LB58**	$9.99

The Revolt of Rabbi Morris Cohen
Exploring the Passion & Piety of a Modern-day Pharisee
—Anthony Cardinale

A brilliant school psychologist, Rabbi Morris Cohen went on a one-man strike to protest the systematic mislabeling of slow learning pupils as "Learning Disabled" (to extract special education money from the state). His disciplinary hearing, based on the transcript, is a hilarious read! This effusive, garrulous man with an irresistible sense of humor lost his job, but achieved a major historic victory causing the reform of the billion-dollar special education program. Enter into the mind of an eighth-generation Orthodox rabbi to see how he deals spiritually with the loss of everything, even the love of his children. This modern-day Pharisee discovered a trusted friend in the author (a born again believer in Jesus) with whom he could openly struggle over Rabbinic Judaism as well as the concept of Jesus (Yeshua) as Messiah. 320 pages.

Paperback	978-1936716722	**LB92**	$19.99

Stories of Yeshua
—Jim Reimann, Illustrator Julia Filipone-Erez

Children's Bible Storybook with four stories about Yeshua (Jesus).
Yeshua is Born: The Bethlehem Story based on Lk 1:26-35 & 2:1-20; *Yeshua and Nicodemus in Jerusalem* based on Jn 3:1-16; *Yeshua Loves the Little Children of the World* based on Matthew 18:1–6 & 19:13–15; *Yeshua is Alive-The Empty Tomb in Jerusalem* based on Matthew 26:17-56, Jn 19:16-20:18, Lk 24:50-53. Ages 3-7, 48 pages.

Paperback	978-1936716685	**LB89**	$14.99

To the Ends of the Earth – How the First Jewish Followers of Yeshua Transformed the Ancient World
— Dr. Jeffrey Seif

Everyone knows that the first followers of Yeshua were Jews, and that Christianity was very Jewish for the first 50 to 100 years. It's a known fact that there were many congregations made up mostly of Jews, although the false perception today is, that in the second century they disappeared. Dr. Seif reveals the truth of what happened to them and how these early Messianic Jews influenced and transformed the behavior of the known world at that time. 171 pages

Paperback	978-1936716463	**LB83**	$17.99

Jewish Roots and Foundations of the Scriptures I & II
—John Fischer, Th.D, Ph.D.

An outstanding evangelical leader once said: "There is something shallow about a Christianity that has lost its Jewish roots." A beautiful painting is a careful interweaving of a number of elements. Among other things, there are the background, the foreground and the subject. Discovering the roots of your faith is a little like appreciating the various parts of a painting. In the background is the panorama of preparation and pictures found in the Old Testament. In the foreground is the landscape and light of the first century Jewish setting. All of this is intricately connected with and highlights the subject—which becomes the flowering of all these aspects—the coming of God to earth and what that means for us. Discovering and appreciating your roots in this way broadens, deepens and enriches your faith and your understanding of Scripture. This audio is 32 hours of live class instruction - audio is clear and easy to understand.

9781936716623   **LCD03 / LCD04** $49.99 each

The Gospels in their Jewish Context
—John Fischer, Th.D, Ph.D.

An examination of the Jewish background and nature of the Gospels in their contemporary political, cultural and historical settings, emphasizing each gospel's special literary presentation of Yeshua, and highlighting the cultural and religious contexts necessary for understanding each of the gospels. 32 hours of audio/video instruction on MP3-DVD and pdf of syllabus.

978-1936716241   **LCD01** $49.99

The Epistles from a Jewish Perspective
—John Fischer, Th.D, Ph.D.

An examination of the relationship of Rabbi Shaul (the Apostle Paul) and the Apostles to their Jewish contemporaries and environment; surveys their Jewish practices, teaching, controversy with the religious leaders, and many critical passages, with emphasis on the Jewish nature, content, and background of these letters. 32 hours of audio/video instruction on MP3-DVD and pdf of syllabus.

978-1936716258   **LCD02** $49.99

The Red Heifer *A Jewish Cry for Messiah*
—Anthony Cardinale

Award-winning journalist and playwright Anthony Cardinale has traveled extensively in Israel, and recounts here his interviews with Orthodox rabbis, secular Israelis, and Palestinian Arabs about the current search for a red heifer by Jewish radicals wishing to rebuild the Temple and bring the Messiah. These real-life interviews are interwoven within an engaging and dramatic fictional portrayal of the diverse people of Israel and how they would react should that red heifer be found. Readers will find themselves in the Land, where they can hear learned rabbis and ordinary Israelis talking about the red heifer and dealing with all the related issues and the imminent coming and identity of Messiah. 341 pages

Paperback   978-1936716470   **LB79** $19.99

The Borough Park Papers
—Multiple Authors

As you read the New Testament, you "overhear" debates first-century Messianic Jews had about critical issues, e.g. Gentiles being "allowed" into the Messianic kingdom (Acts 15). Similarly, you're now invited to "listen in" as leading twenty-first century Messianic Jewish theologians discuss critical issues facing us today. Some ideas may not fit into your previously held pre-suppositions or pre-conceptions. Indeed, you may find some paradigm shifting in your thinking. We want to share the thoughts of these thinkers with you, our family in the Messiah.

Symposium I:
The Gospel and the Jewish People
248 pages, Paperback   978-1936716593   **LB84** $39.95

Symposium II:
The Deity of Messiah and the Mystery of God
211 pages, Paperback   978-1936716609   **LB85** $39.95

Symposium III:
How Jewish Should the Messianic Community Be?
Paperback   978-1936716616   **LB86** $39.95

Passion for Israel: *A Short History of the Evangelical Church's Support of Israel and the Jewish People*
—Dan Juster

History reveals a special commitment of Christians to the Jews as God's still elect people, but the terrible atrocities committed against the Jews by so-called Christians have overshadowed the many good deeds that have been performed. This important history needs to be told to help heal the wounds and to inspire more Christians to stand together in support of Israel. 84 pages

Paperback   978-1936716401   **LB78** $9.99

On The Way to Emmaus: *Searching the Messianic Prophecies*
—Dr. Jacques Doukhan

An outstanding compilation of the most critical Messianic prophecies by a renowned conservative Christian Scholar, drawing on material from the Bible, Rabbinic sources, Dead Sea Scrolls, and more. 217 pages

Paperback   978-1936716432   **LB80** $14.99

Yeshua *A Guide to the Real Jesus and the Original Church*
—Dr. Ron Moseley

Opens up the history of the Jewish roots of the Christian faith. Illuminates the Jewish background of Yeshua and the Church and never flinches from showing "Jesus was a Jew, who was born, lived, and died, within first century Judaism." Explains idioms in the New Testament. Endorsed by Dr. Brad Young and Dr. Marvin Wilson. 213 pages.

Paperback   978-1880226681   **LB29** $12.99

Gateways to Torah *Joining the Ancient Conversation on the Weekly Portion*
—Rabbi Russell Resnik

From before the days of Messiah until today, Jewish people have read from and discussed a prescribed portion of the Pentateuch each week. Now, a Messianic Jewish Rabbi, Russell Resnik, brings another perspective on the Torah, that of a Messianic Jew. 246 pages.

Paperback	978-1880226889	**LB42**	$15.99

Creation to Completion *A Guide to Life's Journey from the Five Books of Moses*
—Rabbi Russell Resnik

Endorsed by Coach Bill McCartney, Founder of Promise Keepers & Road to Jerusalem: "Paul urged Timothy to study the Scriptures (2 Tim. 3:16), advising him to apply its teachings to all aspects of his life. Since there was no New Testament then, this rabbi/apostle was convinced that his disciple would profit from studying the Torah, the Five Books of Moses, and the Old Testament. Now, Rabbi Resnik has written a warm devotional commentary that will help you understand and apply the Law of Moses to your life in a practical way." 256 pages

Paperback	978-1880226322	**LB61**	$14.99

Walk Genesis! Walk Exodus! Walk Leviticus! Walk Numbers! Walk Deuteronomy!
Messianic Jewish Devotional Commentaries
—Jeffrey Enoch Feinberg, Ph.D.

Using the weekly synagogue readings, Dr. Jeffrey Feinberg has put together some very valuable material in his "Walk" series. Each section includes a short Hebrew lesson (for the non-Hebrew speaker), key concepts, an excellent overview of the portion, and some practical applications. Can be used as a daily devotional as well as a Bible study tool. Paperback.

Walk Genesis!	238 pages	978-1880226759	**LB34**	$12.99
Walk Exodus!	224 pages	978-1880226872	**LB40**	$12.99
Walk Leviticus!	208 pages	978-1880226926	**LB45**	$12.99
Walk Numbers!	211 pages	978-1880226995	**LB48**	$12.99
Walk Deuteronomy!	231 pages	978-1880226186	**LB51**	$12.99
SPECIAL! Five-book Walk!		5 Book Set **Save $10**	**LK28**	$54.99

Good News According To Matthew
—Dr. Henry Einspruch

English translation with quotations from the Tanakh (Old Testament) capitalized and printed in Hebrew. Helpful notations are included. Lovely black and white illustrations throughout the book. 86 pages.

Paperback	978-1880226025	**LB03**	$4.99
Also available in Yiddish.		**LB02**	$4.99

They Loved the Torah *What Yeshua's First Followers Really Thought About the Law*
—Dr. David Friedman

Although many Jews believe that Paul taught against the Law, this book disproves that notion. An excellent case for his premise that all the first followers of the Messiah were not only Torah-observant, but also desired to spread their love for God's entire Word to the gentiles to whom they preached. 144 pages. Endorsed by Dr. David Stern, Ariel Berkowitz, Rabbi Dr. Stuart Dauermann & Dr. John Fischer.

Paperback	978-1880226940	**LB47**	$9.99

The Distortion *2000 Years of Misrepresenting the Relationship Between Jesus the Messiah and the Jewish People*
—Dr. John Fischer & Dr. Patrice Fischer

Did the Jews kill Jesus? Did they really reject him? With the rise of global anti–Semitism, it is important to understand what the Gospels teach about the relationship between Jewish people and their Messiah. 2000 years of distortion have made this difficult. Learn how the distortion began and continues to this day and what you can do to change it. 126 pages. Endorsed by Dr. Ruth Fleischer, Rabbi Russell Resnik, Dr. Daniel C. Juster, Dr. Michael Rydelnik.

Paperback	978-1880226254	**LB54**	$11.99

eBooks Now Available!
Versions available for your favorite reader

Visit www.messianicjewish.net for direct links to these readers for each available eBook.

God's Appointed Times *A Practical Guide to Understanding and Celebrating the Biblical Holidays* – **New Edition.**
—Rabbi Barney Kasdan

The Biblical Holy Days teach us about the nature of God and his plan for mankind, and can be a source of God's blessing for all believers–Jews and Gentiles–today. Includes historical background, traditional Jewish observance, New Testament relevance, and prophetic significance, plus music, crafts and holiday recipes. 145 pages.

English - Paperback	978-1880226353	**LB63**	$12.99
Spanish - Paperback	978-1880226391	**LB59**	$12.99

God's Appointed Customs *A Messianic Jewish Guide to the Biblical Lifecycle and Lifestyle*
— Rabbi Barney Kasdan

Explains how biblical customs are often the missing key to unlocking the depths of Scripture. Discusses circumcision, the Jewish wedding, and many more customs mentioned in the New Testament. Companion to *God's Appointed Times*. 170 pages.

English - Paperback	978-1880226636	**LB26**	$12.99
Spanish - Paperback	978-1880226551	**LB60**	$12.99

Celebrations of the Bible *A Messianic Children's Curriculum*

Did you know that each Old Testament feast or festival finds its fulfillment in the New? They enrich the lives of people who experience and enjoy them. Our popular curriculum for children is in a brand new, user-friendly format. The lay-flat at binding allows you to easily reproduce handouts and worksheets. Celebrations of the Bible has been used by congregations, Sunday schools, ministries, homeschoolers, and individuals to teach children about the biblical festivals. Each of these holidays are presented for Preschool (2-K), Primary (Grades 1-3), Junior (Grades 4-6), and Children's Worship/Special Services. 208 pages.

Paperback	978-1880226261	**LB55**	$24.99

Passover: *The Key That Unlocks the Book of Revelation*
—Daniel C. Juster, Th.D.

Is there any more enigmatic book of the Bible than Revelation? Controversy concerning its meaning has surrounded it back to the first century. Today, the arguments continue. Yet, Dan Juster has given us the key that unlocks the entire book—the events and circumstances of the Passover/Exodus. By interpreting Revelation through the lens of Exodus, Dan Juster provides a unified overview that helps us read Revelation as it was always meant to be read, as a drama of spiritual conflict, deliverance, and above all, worship. He also shows how this final drama, fulfilled in Messiah, resonates with the Torah and all of God's Word. — Russ Resnik, Executive Director, Union of Messianic Jewish Congregations.

Paperback	978-1936716210	**LB74**	$10.99

The Messianic Passover Haggadah
Revised and Updated
—Rabbi Barry Rubin and Steffi Rubin.

Guides you through the traditional Passover seder dinner, step-by-step. Not only does this observance remind us of our rescue from Egyptian bondage, but, we remember Messiah's last supper, a Passover seder. The theme of redemption is seen throughout the evening. What's so unique about our Haggadah is the focus on Yeshua (Jesus) the Messiah and his teaching, especially on his last night in the upper room. 36 pages.

English - Paperback	978-1880226292	**LB57**	$4.99
Spanish - Paperback	978-1880226599	**LBSP01**	$4.99

The Messianic Passover Seder Preparation Guide
Includes recipes, blessings and songs. 19 pages.

English - Paperback	978-1880226247	**LB10**	$2.99
Spanish - Paperback	978-1880226728	**LBSP02**	$2.99

The Sabbath *Entering God's Rest*
—Barry Rubin & Steffi Rubin

Even if you've never celebrated Shabbat before, this book will guide you into the rest God has for all who would enter in—Jews and non-Jews. Contains prayers, music, recipes; in short, everything you need to enjoy the Sabbath, even how to observe havdalah, the closing ceremony of the Sabbath. Also discusses the Saturday or Sunday controversy. 48 pages.

Paperback	978-1880226742	**LB32**	$6.99

Havdalah *The Ceremony that Completes the Sabbath*
—Dr. Neal & Jamie Lash

The Sabbath ends with this short, yet equally sweet ceremony called havdalah (separation). This ceremony reminds us to be a light and a sweet fragrance in this world of darkness as we carry the peace, rest, joy and love of the Sabbath into the work week. 28 pages.

Paperback	978-1880226605	**LB69**	$4.99

Dedicate and Celebrate!
A Messianic Jewish Guide to Hanukkah
—Barry Rubin & Family

Hanukkah means "dedication" — a theme of significance for Jews and Christians. Discussing its historical background, its modern-day customs, deep meaning for all of God's people, this little book covers all the how-tos! Recipes, music, and prayers for lighting the menorah, all included! 32 pages.

Paperback	978-1880226834	**LB36**	$4.99

The Conversation
An Intimate Journal of the Emmaus Encounter
—Judy Salisbury

"Then beginning with Moses and with all the prophets, He explained to them the things concerning Himself in all the Scriptures." Luke 24:27
If you've ever wondered what that conversation must have been like, this captivating book takes you there.
"The Conversation brings to life that famous encounter between the two disciples and our Lord Jesus on the road to Emmaus. While it is based in part on an imaginative reconstruction, it is filled with the throbbing pulse of the excitement of the sensational impact that our Lord's resurrection should have on all of our lives." ~ Dr. Walter Kaiser President Emeritus Gordon-Conwell Theological Seminary. Hardcover 120 pages.

Hardcover	978-1936716173	**LB73**	$14.99
Paperback	978-1936716364	**LB77**	$9.99

Growing to Maturity
A Messianic Jewish Discipleship Guide
—Daniel C. Juster, Th.D.

This discipleship series presents first steps of understanding and spiritual practice, tailored for the Jewish believer. It's purpose is to aid the believer in living according to Yeshua's will as a disciple, one who has learned the example of his teacher. The course is structured according to recent advances in individualized educational instruction. Discipleship is serious business and the material is geared for serious study and reflection. Each chapter is divided into short sections followed by study questions. 256 pages.

Paperback	978-1936716227	**LB75**	$19.99

Growing to Maturity Primer: *A Messianic Jewish Discipleship Workbook*
—Daniel C. Juster, Th.D.

A basic book of material in question and answer form. Usable by everyone. 60 pages.

Paperback	978-0961455507	**TB16**	$7.99

Conveying Our Heritage A Messianic Jewish Guide to Home Practice
—Daniel C. Juster, Th.D. Patricia A. Juster

Throughout history the heritage of faith has been conveyed within the family and the congregation. The first institution in the Bible is the family and only the family can raise children with an adequate appreciation of our faith and heritage. This guide exists to help families learn how to pass on the heritage of spiritual Messianic Jewish life. Softcover, 86 pages

Paperback	978-1936716739	**LB93**	$8.99

That They May Be One *A Brief Review of Church Restoration Movements and Their Connection to the Jewish People*
—Daniel Juster, Th.D

Something prophetic and momentous is happening. The Church is finally fully grasping its relationship to Israel and the Jewish people. Author describes the restoration movements in Church history and how they connected to Israel and the Jewish people. Each one contributed in some way—some more, some less—toward the ultimate unity between Jews and Gentiles. Predicted in the Old Testament and fulfilled in the New, Juster believes this plan of God finds its full expression in Messianic Judaism. He may be right. See what you think as you read *That They May Be One*. 100 pages.

| Paperback | 978-1880226711 | **LB71** | $9.99 |

The Greatest Commandment
How the Sh'ma Leads to More Love in Your Life
—Irene Lipson

"What is the greatest commandment?" Yeshua was asked. His reply—"Hear, O Israel, the Lord our God, the Lord is one, and you are to love Adonai your God with all your heart, with all your soul, with all your understanding, and all your strength." A superb book explaining each word so the meaning can be fully grasped and lived. Endorsed by Elliot Klayman, Susan Perlman, & Robert Stearns. 175 pages.

| Paperback | 978-1880226360 | **LB65** | $12.99 |

Blessing the King of the Universe
Transforming Your Life Through the Practice of Biblical Praise
—Irene Lipson

Insights into the ancient biblical practice of blessing God are offered clearly and practically. With examples from Scripture and Jewish tradition, this book teaches the biblical formula used by men and women of the Bible, including the Messiah; points to new ways and reasons to praise the Lord; and explains more about the Jewish roots of the faith. Endorsed by Rabbi Barney Kasdan, Dr. Mitch Glaser, & Rabbi Dr. Dan Cohn-Sherbok. 144 pages.

| Paperback | 978-1880226797 | **LB53** | $11.99 |

You Bring the Bagels, I'll Bring the Gospel
Sharing the Messiah with Your Jewish Neighbor
Revised Edition—Now with Study Questions
—Rabbi Barry Rubin

This "how-to-witness-to-Jewish-people" book is an orderly presentation of everything you need to share the Messiah with a Jewish friend. Includes Messianic prophecies, Jewish objections to believing, sensitivities in your witness, words to avoid. A "must read" for all who care about the Jewish people. Good for individual or group study. Used in Bible schools. Endorsed by Harold A. Sevener, Dr. Walter C. Kaiser, Dr. Erwin J. Kolb and Dr. Arthur F. Glasser. 253 pages, Paperback.

| English | 978-1880226650 | **LB13** | $12.99 |
| Te Tengo Buenas Noticias | 978-0829724103 | **OBSP02** | $14.99 |

Making Eye Contact With God
A Weekly Devotional for Women
—Terri Gillespie

What kind of eyes do you have? Are they downcast and sad? Are they full of God's joy and passion? See yourself through the eyes of God. Using real life anecdotes, combined with scripture, the author reveals God's heart for women everywhere, as she softly speaks of the ways in which women see God. Endorsed by prominent authors: Dr. Angela Hunt, Wanda Dyson and Kathryn Mackel. 247 pages.

Hardcover	978-1880226513	**LB68**	$19.99

Divine Reversal
The Transforming Ethics of Jesus
—Rabbi Russell Resnik

In the Old Testament, God often reversed the plans of man. Yeshua's ethics continue this theme. Following his path transforms one's life from within, revealing the source of true happiness, forgiveness, reconciliation, fidelity and love. From the introduction, "As a Jewish teacher, Jesus doesn't separate matters of theology from practice. His teaching is consistently practical, ethical, and applicable to real life, even two thousand years after it was originally given." Endorsed by Jonathan Bernis, Dr. Daniel C. Juster, Dr. Jeffrey L. Seif, and Dr Darrell Bock. 206 pages

Paperback	978-1880226803	**LB72**	$12.99

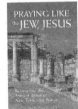

Praying Like the Jew, Jesus
Recovering the Ancient Roots of New Testament Prayer
—Dr. Timothy P. Jones

This eye-opening book reveals the Jewish background of many of Yeshua's prayers. Historical vignettes "transport" you to the times of Yeshua so you can grasp the full meaning of Messiah's prayers. Unique devotional thoughts and meditations, presented in down-to-earth language, provide inspiration for a more meaningful prayer life and help you draw closer to God. Endorsed by Mark Galli, James W. Goll, Rev. Robert Stearns, James F. Strange, and Dr. John Fischer. 144 pages.

Paperback	978-1880226285	**LB56**	$9.99

Growing Your Olive Tree Marriage *A Guide for Couples*
from Two Traditions
—David J. Rudolph

One partner is Jewish; the other is Christian. Do they celebrate Hanukkah, Christmas or both? Do they worship in a church or a synagogue? How will the children be raised? This is the first book from a biblical perspective that addresses the concerns of intermarried couples, offering a godly solution. Includes highlights of interviews with intermarried couples. Endorsed by Walter C. Kaiser, Jr., Rabbi Dan Cohn-Sherbok, Jonathan Settel, Dr. Mitchell Glaser & Natalie Sirota. 224 pages.

Paperback	978-1880226179	**LB50**	$12.99

In Search of the Silver Lining *Where is God in the Midst of Life's Storms?*
—Jerry Gramckow

When faced with suffering, what are your choices? Storms have always raged. And people have either perished in their wake or risen above the tempests, shaping history by their responses...new storms are on the horizon. How will we deal with them? How will we shape history or those who follow us? The answer lies in how we view God in the midst of the storms. Endorsed by Joseph C. Aldrich, Ray Beeson, Dr. Daniel Juster. 176 pages.

| Paperback | 978-1880226865 | **LB39** | $10.99 |

The Voice of the Lord *Messianic Jewish Daily Devotional*
—Edited by David J. Rudolph

Brings insight into the Jewish Scriptures—both Old and New Testaments. Twenty-two prominent Messianic contributors provide practical ways to apply biblical truth. Start your day with this unique resource. Explanatory notes. Perfect companion to the Complete Jewish Bible (see page 2). Endorsed by Edith Schaeffer, Dr. Arthur F. Glaser, Dr. Michael L. Brown, Mitch Glaser and Moishe Rosen. 416 pages.

| Paperback | 9781880226704 | **LB31** | $19.99 |

Kingdom Relationships *God's Laws for the Community of Faith*
—Dr. Ron Moseley

Dr. Ron Moseley's Yeshua: A Guide to the Real Jesus and the Original Church has taught thousands of people about the Jewishness of not only Yeshua, but of the first followers of the Messiah.
In this work, Moseley focuses on the teaching of Torah -- the Five Books of Moses -- tapping into truths that greatly help modern-day members of the community of faith. 64 pages.

| Paperback | 978-1880226841 | **LB37** | $8.99 |

Mutual Blessing *Discovering the Ultimate Destiny of Creation*
—Daniel C. Juster

To truly love as God loves is to see the wonder and richness of the distinct differences in all of creation and his natural order of interdependence. This is the way to mutual blessing and the discovery of the ultimate destiny of creation. Learn how to become enriched and blessed as you enrich and bless others and all that is around you! Softcover, 135 pages.

| Paperback | 978-1936716746 | **LB94** | $9.99 |

Train Up A Child *Successful Parenting For The Next Generation*
—Dr. Daniel L. Switzer

The author, former principal of Ets Chaiyim Messianic Jewish Day School, and father of four, combines solid biblical teaching with Jewish sources on child raising, focusing on the biblical holy days, giving fresh insight into fulfilling the role of parent. 188 pages. Endorsed by Dr. David J. Rudolph, Paul Lieberman, and Dr. David H. Stern.

| Paperback | 978-1880226377 | **LB64** | $12.99 |

Fire on the Mountain - *Past Renewals, Present Revivals and the Coming Return of Israel*
—Dr. Louis Goldberg

The term "revival" is often used to describe a person or congregation turning to God. Is this something that "just happens," or can it be brought about? Dr. Louis Goldberg, author and former professor of Hebrew and Jewish Studies at Moody Bible Institute, examines real revivals that took place in Bible times and applies them to today. 268 pages.

Paperback	978-1880226858 **LB38**	$15.99

Voices of Messianic Judaism *Confronting Critical Issues Facing a Maturing Movement*
—General Editor Rabbi Dan Cohn-Sherbok

Many of the best minds of the Messianic Jewish movement contributed their thoughts to this collection of 29 substantive articles. Challenging questions are debated: The involvement of Gentiles in Messianic Judaism? How should outreach be accomplished? Liturgy or not? Intermarriage? 256 pages.

Paperback	978-1880226933 **LB46**	$15.99

The Enduring Paradox *Exploratory Essays in Messianic Judaism*
—General Editor Dr. John Fischer

Yeshua and his Jewish followers began a new movement—Messianic Judaism—2,000 years ago. In the 20th century, it was reborn. Now, at the beginning of the 21st century, it is maturing. Twelve essays from top contributors to the theology of this vital movement of God, including: Dr. Walter C. Kaiser, Dr. David H. Stern, and Dr. John Fischer. 196 pages.

Paperback	978-1880226902 **LB43**	$13.99

The World To Come *A Portal to Heaven on Earth*
—Derek Leman

An insightful book, exposing fallacies and false teachings surrounding this extremely important subject... paints a hopeful picture of the future and dispels many non-biblical notions. Intriguing chapters: Magic and Desire, The Vision of the Prophets, Hints of Heaven, Horrors of Hell, The Drama of the Coming Ages. Offers a fresh, but old, perspective on the world to come, as it interacts with the prophets of Israel and the Bible. 110 pages.

Paperback	978-1880226049 **LB67**	$9.99

Hebrews Through a Hebrew's Eyes
—Dr. Stuart Sacks

Written to first-century Messianic Jews, this epistle, understood through Jewish eyes, edifies and encourages all. 119 pages. Endorsed by Dr. R.C. Sproul and James M. Boice.

Paperback	978-1880226612 **LB23**	$10.99

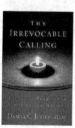

The Irrevocable Calling *Israel's Role As A Light To The Nations*
—Daniel C. Juster, Th.D.

Referring to the chosen-ness of the Jewish people, Paul, the Apostle, wrote "For God's free gifts and his calling are irrevocable" (Rom. 11:29). This messenger to the Gentiles understood the unique calling of his people, Israel. So does Dr. Daniel Juster, President of Tikkun Ministries Int'l. In *The Irrevocable Calling*, he expands Paul's words, showing how Israel was uniquely chosen to bless the world and how these blessings can be enjoyed today. Endorsed by Dr. Jack Hayford, Mike Bickle and Don Finto. 64 pages.

Paperback	978-1880226346	**LB66**	$8.99

Are There Two Ways of Atonement?
—Dr. Louis Goldberg

Here Dr. Louis Goldberg, long-time professor of Jewish Studies at Moody Bible Institute, exposes the dangerous doctrine of Two-Covenant Theology. 32 pages.

Paperback	978-1880226056	**LB12**	$ 4.99

Awakening *Articles and Stories About Jews and Yeshua*
—Arranged by Anna Portnov

Articles, testimonies, and stories about Jewish people and their relationship with God, Israel, and the Messiah. Includes the effective tract, "The Most Famous Jew of All." One of our best anthologies for witnessing to Jewish people. Let this book witness for you! Russian version also available. 110 pages.

English - Paperback	978-1880226094	**LB15**	$ 6.99
Russian - Paperback	978-1880226018	**LB14**	$ 6.99

The Unpromised Land *The Struggle of Messianic Jews Gary and Shirley Beresford*
—Linda Alexander

They felt God calling them to live in Israel, the Promised Land. Wanting nothing more than to live quietly and grow old together in the country of refuge for all Jewish people, little did they suspect what events would follow to try their faith. The fight to make *aliyah*, to claim their rightful inheritance in the Promised Land, became a battle waged not only for themselves, but also for Messianic Jews all over the world that wish to return to the Jewish homeland. Here is the true saga of the Beresford's journey to the land of their forefathers. 216 pages.

Paperback	978-1880226568	**LB19**	$ 9.99